"Adam Gustine writes with the h[...] Immersed in sincerity from Gu[...] repentance, a testament of how [...] God's transformative love. *Becoming a Just Church* provides a biblical approach for churches to seek shalom in their contexts, living as God's demonstration for the world to witness with wonder. Like a hearty Sunday benediction, every chapter should inspire many to live into God's dream of tomorrow for our world right now."

José Humphreys, author of *Seeing Jesus in East Harlem*, pastor of Metro Hope Covenant Church, New York

"There is a generation of white evangelical Christians who are discovering God's beautiful and risky call to seek justice in this world. Unfortunately, many of these younger women and men were discipled in churches where justice was viewed as being either tangential to the gospel or a threat to it. The result is that as they grow close to God's heart for justice, these young Christians often move away from church. *Becoming a Just Church* demonstrates how unnecessary the gap between justice and church is. Rather than being an impediment to justice, Adam contends that our congregations are meant to provide the spiritual formation that matures us into people who don't simply *do* justice but who *are* just. He has written a book that is wise and practical. If we let these pages shape our imaginations, it's possible that generations of Christians will mature within just congregations. And what a hopeful future that would be!"

David Swanson, pastor of New Community Covenant Church, Chicago

"Adam approaches the topic of biblical justice from a position of humility and with the heart of a pastor. For any church looking to embrace God's heart for justice more deeply, you will find *Becoming a Just Church* to be a valuable theological and practical resource."

Daniel Hill, author of *White Awake*, pastor of River City Community Church, Chicago

"*Becoming a Just Church* is not just another book about justice. It's like reading a memoir, a prophetic challenge, and a practical guide all in one. Adam Gustine writes neither from the high vantage point of the ivory tower of academia nor from a chip-on-the-shoulder condescending edge as if to display his superiority. Instead, he writes clearly with a posture of vulnerability and humble confidence rooted in praxis. Adam doesn't merely write about the importance of embodying justice within a local church; he lives it. This book will be helpful for any church or leader who isn't merely interested in doing justice because it's trendy, but instead who is committed to embodying the way of justice for the sake of God and his shalom."

J.R. Briggs, founder of Kairos Partnerships, author of *Fail: Finding Hope and Grace in the Midst of Ministry Failure*

"*Becoming a Just Church* offers us a beautiful and deeply biblical vision of the church as the primary conduit of God's shalom (justice, wholeness, and harmony) invading our broken world. As Adam Gustine humbly shares his own often-faltering journey in discovering the centrality of God's justice for the gospel, he insightfully exposes the various reasons why white American evangelicals in particular tend to overlook this biblical vision, misunderstand God's justice, and frequently end up inadvertently contributing to the very injustice we are supposed to be confronting. *Becoming a Just Church* is a well-written, eye-opening, paradigm-shifting, prophetic and pastoral work that has the potential to fundamentally transform the way readers—and especially white evangelical readers—think about church and engage with issues of justice. If you've ever sensed that the church should be a greater force for transforming society, *read this book!*"

Greg Boyd, senior pastor of Woodland Hills Church, president of reknew.org

"At this time in human history our awareness of a fractured and broken world is unavoidable. The body of Christ was one of Jesus' gifts to our broken world yet the privileged white American church is plagued by partisan divides, a compromised public witness, and the lack of urgency needed to undo injustice's oppression. It is hard to imagine a redemptive way forward for the privileged white American church, but this book reframes the much-needed narrative, digging deep into truth. Refuting cultural lies that keep the American church lulled to sleep and out of the important justice work God is doing in the world. The message of this book is a much-needed wake-up call. The message is a benefit for all Christians but most specifically for white privileged Christians; together we can move toward the repentance, healing, and redemption needed to alleviate injustice."

Michelle Ferrigno Warren, author of *The Power of Proximity*

"Drawing on personal experience and writing from the heart, Adam Gustine shares how the church is called to work for change, justice, and social transformation. *Becoming a Just Church* provides practical steps and guidelines to guide the church toward new life. Gustine's prophetic vision instills hope to lead the next generation of faithful believers."

Grace Ji-Sun Kim, associate professor of theology at Earlham School of Religion, author of *Healing Our Broken Humanity*

"God's church was always intended to be a vehicle for God's shalom. And Gustine helps us dream new dreams about what a church that leans into this calling could look like. He exhorts communities to not just *do* justice but also to embody justice in all aspects of community life. A helpful resource for Christian communities wanting to embody God's shalom in the communities where they are placed."

Nikki Toyama-Szeto, executive director of ESA/The Sider Center

"*Becoming a Just Church* appropriately centers our call to do justice as actual congregations. With pastoral experience and care, Adam Gustine reminds us of our vocation as a prophetic and exilic people seeking shalom. This theologically astute resource is a must-read for evangelical churches, though most American congregations would do well to discuss and discern the significance of this book together."

Drew G. I. Hart, assistant professor of theology at Messiah College, author of *Trouble I've Seen: Changing the Way the Church Views Racism*

"Honestly, this book is now my top priority recommendation to every local church that is seeking to be faithful to God's call for justice. Clearly, we are living in a critical season, and the church needs to take action. But our paradigms for entering this work feel enshrouded in a thick fog of competing options and compartmentalized strategies. Adam Gustine is a prophetic guide for white Christians like me. He cuts to the quick and gets us focused back on first things first. This book leads straight to the root issues of justice, issues that begin with our own need to live out a communal alternative to the broken systems of the world. From this living 'demonstration plot,' we can become an authentic voice that extends God's justice out into the world in tangible ways. I hope churches, seminaries, and faith communities of every variation will buy this book in bulk, assign it for slow reflective reading, and follow it up with serious imaginative engagement."

Paul Sparks, coauthor of *The New Parish*, cofounding director of the Parish Collective

"*Becoming a Just Church* isn't about ramping up your church's outreach activities, nor is it about the problem of injustice 'out there' that needs to be solved. It is about the church becoming who she was always intended to be by God's design: a people who reflect the shalom community of a triune God. Rooted in robust biblical theology that extends into a beautiful shalom-centered ecclesiology, anchored by stories from on-the-ground ministry to fuel our imagination, Adam Gustine draws from his pastoral experience and resources us with the practical wisdom we need to explore what it means to become a just church. Pastoral and prophetic in tone, this will be a gift for both pastors and laypeople alike in a time where we must all examine the question of what it means to be the people of God today."

Juliet Liu, copastor at Life on the Vine Church, editorial director at Missio Alliance

"In *Becoming a Just Church*, Adam calls the church to awaken to its unique ability to be a beacon of hope. He challenges us to no longer sit on the sidelines and complain but to live out the great commandment and allow it to lead us down a path of justice that emanates from a true love for God and our neighbor."

Jonathan Brooks, pastor of Canaan Community Church, author of *Church Forsaken*

"Particularly for white evangelical Christians like me, 'justice' can easily become a fad, a program, or a means to another end. But as Adam Gustine argues in *Becoming a Just Church*, justice is a biblical idea that God intends for the whole church to embody as a community. With careful biblical analysis, practical examples, and a healthy dose of self-awareness, Gustine provides a road map for churches wanting to live out the biblical command to do justly."

Matthew Soerens, US director of Church Mobilization, World Relief, coauthor of *Welcoming the Stranger*

"Adam Gustine is not only a thoughtful author, pastor, friend, and die-hard Notre Dame fan, he is a man committed to leading his church, and churches like yours, into a lifestyle of justice. Drawing on a sound theology, Gustine gently guides us into principled application. For those who want to follow Jesus on the narrow and hard road of church and city—shalom, this book is for you!"

John Teter, author of *The Power of the 72*, senior pastor of Fountain of Life Covenant Church

"I love it when pastors write about justice. Why? Because they keep it on the ground where real people live and struggle. With a genuine pastor's heart and years of experience, Adam Gustine combines a compelling theological vision of God's shalom and a practical way forward for churches to understand and live out that vision in their neighborhoods and beyond. He pulls this off with humility, grace, and grit. That is, far from coming off like he has it all figured out, Gustine offers insights wrought not just from triumphs but also from mistakes. He knows better than most that justice work is a journey. I for one am glad that Gustine is there to walk alongside us."

Al Tizon, executive minister of Serve Globally, author of *Whole and Reconciled*

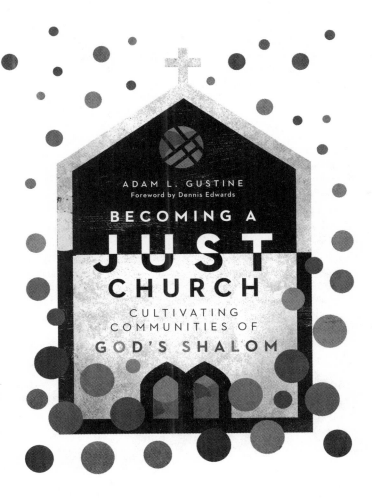

ADAM L. GUSTINE

Foreword by Dennis Edwards

BECOMING A JUST CHURCH

CULTIVATING COMMUNITIES OF

GOD'S SHALOM

IVP Books

An imprint of InterVarsity Press
Downers Grove, Illinois

InterVarsity Press
P.O. Box 1400, Downers Grove, IL 60515-1426
ivpress.com
email@ivpress.com

InterVarsity Press® is the book-publishing division of InterVarsity Christian Fellowship/USA®, a movement of students and faculty active on campus at hundreds of universities, colleges, and schools of nursing in the United States of America, and a member movement of the International Fellowship of Evangelical Students. For information about local and regional activities, visit intervarsity.org.

All Scripture quotations, unless otherwise indicated, are taken from The Holy Bible, New International Version®, NIV®. Copyright © 1973, 1978, 1984, 2011 by Biblica, Inc.™ Used by permission of Zondervan. All rights reserved worldwide. www.zondervan.com. The "NIV" and "New International Version" are trademarks registered in the United States Patent and Trademark Office by Biblica, Inc.™

While any stories in this book are true, some names and identifying information may have been changed to protect the privacy of individuals.

Cover design: David Fassett
Interior design: Daniel van Loon
Images: urban skyline: © CSA Images/Archive / Getty Images
    abstract blue watercolor: © Nottomanv1 / iStock / Getty Images Plus
    white brushstroke background: © Dmytro_Skorobogatov / iStock / Getty Images Plus
    old yellowed paper texture: © ke77kz / iStock / Getty Images Plus
    abstract watercolor pattern: © arborelza / iStock / Getty Images Plus

ISBN 978-0-8308-4151-6 (print)
ISBN 978-0-8308-7340-1 (digital)

Printed in the United States of America ∞

InterVarsity Press is committed to ecological stewardship and to the conservation of natural resources in all our operations. This book was printed using sustainably sourced paper.

Library of Congress Cataloging-in-Publication Data
A catalog record for this book is available from the Library of Congress.

P	21	20	19	18	17	16	15	14	13	12	11	10	9	8	7	6	5	4	3	2	1
Y	36	35	34	33	32	31	30	29	28	27	26	25	24	23	22	21	20	19			

**THIS BOOK IS DEDICATED TO MY KIDS:
JOSIAH, LEVI, AND NINA.**

*My prayer is that the church you come to know and serve is an
evermore faithful reflection of Jesus—the One making us all
whole and putting the broken pieces back together.*

CONTENTS

Foreword by Dennis Edwards   *1*

Introduction   *3*

PART 1: AN ECCLESIOLOGY FOR JUSTICE

1 Justice Isn't an Outreach Strategy   *19*
A Way of Life for the People of God

2 Exiles in the Promised Land   *38*
The Church as Prophetic Alternative

3 Demonstrating Mañana   *55*
The Church as a Parable of God's Intent

4 Gardeners of Shalom   *76*
The Church for Flourishing and Transformation

PART 2: JUSTICE IN OUR CONGREGATIONAL LIFE

5 Low-Ground Church   *99*
Discerning Vision in a High-Ground World

6 Recovering Kinship   *119*
Hospitality as Resistance

7 Finding Common Kingdom Ground   *142*
Discipling People into Shalom Community

8 Worship   *158*
Questions That Drive How We Gather

PART 3: WHAT'S NEXT?

9 Power   *177*
*A Conversation About the Linchpin of Justice
with Juliet Liu and Brandon Green*

Epilogue   *193*
Commence Justice

Acknowledgments   *203*

Notes   *205*

FOREWORD

DENNIS EDWARDS

Adam Gustine has done the church in the United States a great service. *Becoming a Just Church* is one of those rare books possessing the potential to change the way we think about and do Christian ministry. We need to hear what Dr. Gustine has to say because there are way too many "here's how you can have a church like mine" sort of books, written by charming leaders who managed to grow large churches but who try to quantify and perhaps even commodify the grace of God through their books.

I've twice been a church planter (Brooklyn, NY, and Washington, DC) and twice been called to serve established churches (Washington, DC, and Minneapolis, MN). Along my journey of over thirty years in urban ministry, I've become acquainted with books that typically tell the stories of a church's (or a pastor's) success—usually defined as large numbers of people attending weekend worship services. Rarely have I encountered books to help Christians understand that the practice of God's justice is part of Christian discipleship and not merely some program added onto an already overloaded schedule. *Becoming a Just Church* offers a way of thinking for newly planted churches as well as established churches in a variety of settings (i.e., urban, suburban, rural). While Gustine's principles are certainly biblical, they are not merely theoretical; they mirror genuine pastoral realities.

I think that many pastors can relate to people getting fired up over an issue in the news and wondering what the church (or the pastor) will do about it. We find that our passion for justice comes in waves or flares up, depending on the news cycle. Yet God calls his people—in both Testaments of Scripture—to do justly, love mercy, and walk humbly with God. Passion for justice does not have its provenance in any particular political ideology, although it can often feel that way in our polarized society. The Great Commandment—to wholeheartedly love the Lord and love our neighbors—provides the drive for Christian commitment to justice, not the Democratic or Republican parties of the United States.

Becoming a Just Church provides both a theological framework as well as practical guidance on how followers of Jesus can live out the Great Commandment.

INTRODUCTION

I am a liability in the work of justice. I think it's important to just come right out and articulate reality here at the start.

As a white, male, American I carry with me a way of seeing the world—and of engaging in it—that has serious blind spots in the work of pursuing God's shalom. The tangible markers of my privilege have afforded me much in the way of opportunity, network, support systems—even access to capital—and so while I may think I have accomplished this or that of my own accord, the final valuation of my life will reveal that at every step of the way I've been positioned by influences, seen and unseen, to ensure the best possible outcomes. Struggle and tribulation have been infrequent—even absent—from my life. In some ways, I am the model of the American "self-made man" because it's possible for me to believe I am self-made and ignore the reality that I have been profoundly *made* by a culture that is designed to see me succeed.

The same society whose structures created a nearly effortless path for my "success" is also at work in other ways for other folks. For a social status quo to prefer some groups of people (white, male, American, educated, upwardly mobile), it also must push other groups to the margins. But inequality is not easily understandable to someone who has not experienced the back side of privilege. This has been my experience. I had no awareness of systemic

injustice or structural inequality growing up. Injustice and discrimination were things of the past, and the major flare-ups of, say,
racial tension, were not a sign of current reality but of people
refusing to let go of the past. When Rodney King and O.J. Simpson
inflamed cultural moments, which escalated—beyond the stories
themselves—the conversation around race and structural inequality
in America, I lived in a world comfortably distant from those
realities, so I was comfortable in dismissing the protest that emerged
as something unworthy of my time and attention. The world I grew
up in had no imagination for a life we didn't make on our own—we
all have to sleep in the bed we make—and that if we would just try
harder, not make stupid mistakes, and make sure to not be like *those*
people, everyone had a fighting chance to make it. That my high
school classmate Marcus might not go to college had little to do
with his social location—the particulars of where and how we were
born and raised, and opportunities afforded us—just the same as
the fact that I would go to any school I wanted to had little to do
with mine. My success—academic or otherwise—was a reflection
of me as a person. Marcus's future was a reflection of him.

This, I've come to see, is one of the base positions of white
America. What we do with our life is a reflection of our character
and our identity. Because we live in the land of equal opportunity,
what a person makes of themselves is evidence of work ethic, drive,
vision, talent, and so forth. I'm convinced this is why so many of us
are scared to go back to our ten-year high school reunions. If our
decade of postsecondary achievements weren't a determining factor
of whether or not we had value as people, we'd probably all go and
have a good time. Another book maybe . . .

This idea—so central to the white American imagination—is
poison for justice. We who grow up in the waters of white America

are swimming in this poison, and we become toxic. At least I did. I've never waved a Confederate flag at a race rally or systemically defrauded the poor, but I have personally participated in—and benefitted from—a cultural way of life that does. And for most of my life, I had no idea.

My first steps into the world of justice came through my exposure to the global AIDS crisis. I was just out of college and Bono was trying to get Christians to pay attention to the way this disease was ravaging sub-Saharan Africa. I heard his 2006 prayer breakfast sermon; one of the best I've heard on justice. I still catch my breath when I read it.

> God is in the slums, in the cardboard boxes where the poor play house. God is in the silence of a mother who has infected her child with a virus that will end both their lives. God is in the cries heard under the rubble of war. God is in the debris of wasted opportunity and lives, and God is with us if we are with them.[1]

"God is with us if we are with them." I really don't think that any single sentence has ever shattered my life more than this one. It's hard to say why it did because I didn't really have any life experience to corroborate it as true. I think, though, that Truth finds its way into our souls and makes itself at home, even when we don't open the door. At least that's what happened to me. I dove in with both feet. I led a team to Africa, I sat at the bedside of a small boy—the same age as my middle son is today—who wouldn't leave the clinic he was in because of a disease that would claim his life. We worshiped alongside sisters and brothers who were dealing with the most incredibly difficult conditions, facing challenges that I had never dreamed of, and I was simultaneously inspired and mortified. How could this be? How could it be that this kind of suffering existed in the world? (I still had no concrete imagination for an American expression of injustice.)

Coming home from this trip, I found myself wondering how God could allow this to happen. Still laboring under an unrefined, predeterminate worldview, I wondered, *What could God be thinking here?* Until one day, sitting with my mentor and boss, Greg, on our little Christian college campus on the outskirts of Chicago, I was lamenting this serious question, this challenge to my faith. I asked some version of *How could God let . . . ?* and Greg's response changed the trajectory of my life. He said, "Adam, God's already given the world what it needs—the church." He proceeded to talk about how—in hard numbers—the church had every resource needed to address a huge swath of the injustices plaguing our world. Poverty, hunger, clean water, disease, housing, education. The problem wasn't that God didn't care about helping these folks. The problem was that the means God chose to demonstrate justice wasn't working right. The church was blocking the free flow of God's shalom.

So, now fifteen years later, the question is, *Was Greg right?* Was that the answer? You might guess that I do think he is right. I don't think the answer is straightforward, but the intervening decade and a half of ministry—overwhelmingly focused on justice and the church—has proven to me two things: that justice is *central* to the heart of God and his mission in the world, and that the church has not seen it that way for far too long.

After this conversation, I became a crusader for justice. My wife's and my passion for these things eventually led us to move our young family a few times in search of a way to live out of and into the passionate center of our view of the kingdom, that care and concern for justice—focused on the margins—is an inextricable part of a gospel-shaped life.

But despite my newfound zeal, I was still a liability. I just didn't see it. The time it took for me to come to grips with this liability status might have been my biggest blind spot of all. The issue is that I don't automatically assume I am a liability. I was groomed to have faith in myself that I have the answers for any and all questions, problems, or crises that might arise. I believe there's much more messiah than monkey wrench in me.

I've noticed two things about my journey that I find helpful in reflection. One, when I first encountered the reality of injustice, I turned it into an issue of systematic theology. *How could God allow . . . ?* is a super *white* way of reacting to injustice. The notion that the church, and therefore I, might be complicit in the systems of an unjust world was unimaginable. Crazily, it was easier to lay the fault at the feet of God than to wonder if it might mean I've been out of alignment somehow. After all, I was trained to know the problem wasn't me, or in me, it was *out there* somewhere. Because the problem was *out there*, that meant, two, that I needed to fix it. Having noticed the injustice of the world, I was ready to save the day, just give me the chance. And chances I had. And mistakes I made.

Over the last fifteen years of ministry, I've had to come to grips— an ongoing journey to be sure—with the way I keep questions of injustice at arm's length while also jumping in to try to save the day. And over this fifteen years of ministry I've recognized the pattern that, like me, this is pretty normal for many white evangelicals. Injustice is abstracted or taken on as our pet project where we can save the day.

The church I pastored in New York had undertaken some pretty serious new justice initiatives that were innovative within our denomination. Not surprisingly, there was a significant amount of buzz regarding the work we were doing. A magazine called and wanted to feature our story. I granted an interview—very humbly of course—and at the end of the interview the writer said we needed to schedule a photo shoot. A few days later the photographer —who'd shot spreads with Eli Manning—showed up and began taking pictures. We spent hours getting different shots, but throughout the shoot he and his assistant kept saying, "We still need to get the hero shot." I had no idea what they were talking about until, at the very end, they sent everyone home but me and began taking my photo, alone. Then it hit me. This was the hero shot. That makes me . . . the hero.

It's probably bad to believe your own press, but in this case it was pretty easy. I had come to this congregation when it was at the end of an extreme season of crisis and we were leveling out. We were getting healthy. We were engaging in ministry that lined up with God's heart for justice. None of this would have happened if I hadn't been there *making* it happen. I was the hero!

I never would have admitted it, but I had fallen into the trap—so consistent with white American evangelicalism—of being blind to the fact that I was part of the problem while also believing I was the only solution. This was not a new phenomenon for me, but it was a new degree of intensity.

While I was pastoring there, I enrolled in a doctor of ministry program at what is now Missio Seminary in Philadelphia. I was the only white American in my urban-intercultural cohort, which was led by the late Dr. Manny Ortiz and Dr. Sue Baker. The vast majority of the folks in my cohort were black, bivocational pastors who had labored in the difficult neighborhoods of north Philly for decades. I was unprepared for that experience. It might have been one of the most challenging experiences of my life, but it is a grace upon grace that God put me in the midst of these saints for that season.

The first day of class, Dr. Ortiz—he asked us to call him Manny—started talking about what he called the *hermeneutics of repentance*. He drew a descending spiral on the board and said that while we usually come to the text of Scripture in search of better answers, the work of justice—especially in urban and intercultural contexts—required a different approach. Instead of better answers, we needed better questions. These questions drive us *downward*, deeper, yes, but also to the realization that we've been asking the wrong questions all along. At first, this came across like a clever way to talk about the same old topic of hermeneutics, but I've realized this is another major breaking point for folks like me. We need better questions, he asserted, because the quest for *answers* makes us arrogant. The search for the better *question* is fundamentally about repentance. The hermeneutic of repentance says, "I'm so blind I don't even know the question to ask." Of course, we learn through this way of approaching the text, but the point was that hermeneutics is an exercise of discipleship, of becoming a different kind of person, and that requires repentance.

I couldn't keep my grip on my identity as a *hero* and embrace a hermeneutic of repentance. This cohort changed my life because it was an eighteen-month immersion in the hermeneutic of repentance. These were sisters and brothers who loved me deeply but challenged me greatly. They graciously exposed my blindness to injustice—even as I sought to write about it—and helped me ask the better question. Manny always used to say, "I think you're very nearly there." He always said *nearly*; I apparently still haven't arrived, and I think about those words often. He challenged me to keep pushing into my blind spots as a way of continuing to probe God's heart for the world and what it means to be the church.

The white evangelical church in America is in desperate need of Manny Ortiz. It makes me sad to think he is no longer with us. But his hermeneutic of repentance is still here, and we need that as well. Without the hermeneutic of repentance, I will always be a hopeless liability in the work of seeking God's justice. With it, I truly believe *I* can be mitigated a bit so that God's shalom might flow out into the world through me.

Becoming a Just Church is an invitation to a hermeneutic of repentance. Many of the topics we cover in this conversation are the fruit of work that took root in the classroom with Manny and in the local church spaces I've been graciously entrusted to pastor. The topics this book covers are admittedly not always easy to embrace. They represent a critique of the way the white evangelical church in America particularly has missed—and continues to miss—the mark on justice. I poke and prod in some sensitive areas of church life, but I do so from the sincere desire that we would together learn to ask better questions.

Over time, I've come to see that if you come to these conversations as I did (and probably still do) abstractly or messianically, then the conversation I'm hoping to provoke will likely create a significant strain on our relationship. But from the vantage point of being passionate about questions that drive us to repentance—not only giving us insight but making us more *faithful* along the way—I hope you will join me in seeing these conversations as a kind of freedom to be the kind of people God has always envisioned us to be. I don't claim to capture that vision well, I just know that the deeper I press into God's heart for justice, the more I experience God's life and freedom.

I don't think it comes as a surprise to note that the record on justice is spotty at best for white evangelicals. It has not been part of our normative framework for thinking about the gospel and the mission of the church. Beyond that, justice issues often get framed as *liberal*, making it difficult to have nuanced conversations about modern-day injustice at the level of the local evangelical congregation. In the main, the history of evangelicalism in the United States is evidence of our leeriness if not outright opposition to the pursuit of justice. In 1947, Carl F. H. Henry, the first editor of *Christianity Today*, lamented this reality: "It remains a question whether one can be perpetually indifferent to the problems of social justice and international order, and develop a wholesome personal ethics."[2] Seventy years ago the problem of a disconnect between justice and the lived faithfulness of evangelicals in the United States was a most pressing concern. Sadly, not much has changed.

Our current reality is such that evangelical justice seekers have largely become a sidelined people. Most evangelicals who have a passion to seek the shalom of God in the world have found that their local congregation is indifferent or antagonistic to that desire. In some rare cases this congregational marginalization looks like an often-overlooked justice team, but that is probably an exception rather than the rule. The most likely scenario is that justice-minded evangelicals have learned that the local evangelical congregation is not a safe space to work out those passions.

It is not surprising, then, that this antagonism parallels the rise of evangelical parachurch organizations focused on issues of justice. Understandably these folks, feeling unwanted in local congregations, have increasingly gravitated toward the more proactive organizations and movements that have sprung up along the way both as a way of giving expression to their deepest passion and as a way of making sense of their understanding of Jesus.

Thus, most of the major justice initiatives of the last generation have been outsourced by the local church. Urbana Student Missions Conference, World Relief, World Vision, International Justice Mission, Christian Community Development Association, Sojourners, and Evangelicals for Social Action are just a few of the incredibly powerful evangelical movements for justice that have generated enormous momentum and have helped mobilize a generation of Christians around the cause of justice.

If you spend much time in these circles, as I have, it is stunning to note how often people articulate a sense of family and homecoming when describing their experience of affiliation with these parachurch organizations. Over time, these groups have started to function as *ekklēsia* (church) for the justice-minded Christians who have experienced displacement from congregational life. I suppose this is a kind of double-edged sword. On the one hand, I am thankful for groups that create the spaces for followers of Jesus to work out their worldview into action in a safe and supportive community.

On the other, isn't this reality a tragedy? Isn't the fact that these organizations function as safe havens *from the local church* a devastating critique of the kind of people we have become? Justice organizations play a valuable and needed role in the world without question, but I mourn the role they are also required to play in the lives of many justice-minded evangelicals today because it evidences the severe deficiency of our local, embodied ecclesiology related to justice.

WHAT IF THERE WAS A WAY FORWARD?

Becoming a Just Church is not just a critique of the current realities. Instead, in this book I aim to offer a vision for how the local congregation might regain its foothold in the work of justice and the pursuit of God's shalom. In suggesting that there is a way forward, I suppose I am tipping my hand that I am an idealist when it comes to the local church. I cannot escape the reality that God intends for the kingdom mission to work in and through the church.

That the *missio Dei* extends into the world through the local church is an exceedingly common sentiment these days in evangelicalism. There is a danger here, namely, that saying so can actually function to allow us to perpetuate our evangelical status quo without careful examination and reformation. In many cases, I experience it to be the case that this belief works to cosign our brokenness rather than make our knees quake in fear that the God of all creation would intend to work out the purposes of cosmic reconciliation and renewal through us.

I contend that the way we resist allowing this theological reality to function like a cliché is to be rigorously committed to self-examination as we lean into the reality of being the primary instrument of God's purposes in the world today. If local expressions of the body of Christ are going to live into the fullness of God's vision for the church, specifically as it relates to the pursuit of justice, much will need to change. And it will probably start with repentance.

HOW TO READ *BECOMING A JUST CHURCH*

This book is for anyone, but I write primarily with white American evangelicals in mind. I hope that this creates a lot of conversation in many circles about the nature of the church and what it means to be a people in pursuit of God's shalom. The *fact* is that I am a white American evangelical, so to write for any other group would be an overstep and presumptive. I'm praying that for justice-minded folks—evangelical, evangelical-ish, or other—this book is refreshing and maybe challenges you to reconsider your conviction related to the necessity of the local church. For those of us who have grown up in white evangelical spaces, I'm praying this book is not just an accurate description of reality but is practically helpful in our common passion to be the church God has us on earth to be.

A word about my use of terms. *Justice* is a slippery word that gets used broadly in a variety of unhelpful ways. Without taking the time to develop a complete biblical theology of justice, let me say that justice refers to the presence of God's shalom. That is, God's wholeness where, as some say, nothing is missing and nothing is broken.[3] This comprehensive reality involves every arena of life and is, in my estimation, the notion Jesus is referring to when he said he came to bring abundant life. Abundant, flourishing, thriving life for people and communities as defined by the story of Scripture where what has been broken because of sin is restored, renewed, and reconciled by God in Christ. That is shalom, and the presence of shalom means that justice has taken root in the world.

The terms *justice* and *shalom* are used interchangeably to refer to the reality of God's intentions being realized in concrete ways in the world. There is an interplay between the eschatological reality of God's shalom and justice and the work of God's people in pursuing, living into, those realities in day-to-day life.

Regarding the structure of the book. The intention is to generate a conversation that will aid local congregations in *reimagining their life together* in a way that creates the possibility for *becoming a just people* as they seek to *do justice* in the world. While not a step-by-step guide, the book is structured to provide definition to the ongoing discernment happening in congregations around the role of justice in their common life.

Part one is focused on unpacking a theologically rooted vision for justice in and through the local congregation. These first chapters are about the identity of the church and ask the question, *What does it mean to be the church?* through the lens of justice and God's shalom. These chapters aim to bridge the gap between strong ecclesiology and the church's witness against injustice. The fourth chapter in part one focuses on what the church should be for in the world. We need new ways to think about and act out *what it means to be for shalom in the world,* namely, flourishing and transformation.

Part two seeks to build on the theological vision of part one by engaging the concrete arena of congregational life and asking hard questions about the extent to which God's justice permeates those spaces. Examining the way we discern vision and direction, build community, disciple Christians, and gather for worship helps us gain a better sense of the way justice can become an embodied reality for our congregational life.

Part three asks, *What's next?* in two ways. First, the question of power. Without a serious examination of power—and the way it corrupts the possibility of shalom—all of our other efforts will be for naught. I'm grateful to my friends Juliet Liu and Brandon Green—two of the most thoughtful and passionate pastors I've ever met—for contributing their insights to this chapter. And then a closing word about public justice. I didn't write this book to be a primer on the public work of justice. I have been incredibly fortunate to work alongside people who practice the work of public justice by directly confronting systems of oppression in their day-to-day lives. They are the voices we should hear and the stories we should trust on these issues. My only hope in closing with those words is to point us again to hearing the voices of the often ignored, particularly for us in the white evangelical church.

I hope that no matter where your church sits on the spectrum of seeking justice, you (as a pastor, leader, or layperson) will find it helpful in the discernment of the critical questions facing us in the church and as the church in society. May God use our way of life together as an expression of the kingdom and as a signpost of a world being made new again in Jesus.

PART 1

AN ECCLESIOLOGY
FOR JUSTICE

1

JUSTICE ISN'T AN OUTREACH STRATEGY

A WAY OF LIFE FOR THE PEOPLE OF GOD

A few years ago I was involved with developing an immigrant legal ministry. Our church, located in a first-generation immigrant neighborhood, saw this as a tangible way to care for our neighbors and connect to our community. At the time it was still unusual for a local church to do this kind of work, so start-up required quite a bit of vision casting and support raising. As we cast vision broadly for this legal center, we regularly sold this ministry initiative to the larger evangelical world with a vision of evangelizing "lost" immigrants. We marketed the idea this way because of our hunch that evangelicals generally had little imagination for a legal clinic that wasn't in its essence a cleverly disguised evangelism and church-growth strategy. We did this without regard to whether the populations we served might in fact already be Christian, and without asking if the work of providing this pathway within the US immigration system might be a worthy end on its own. We hadn't planned on creating a dynamic in which the success of a *legal* clinic would ultimately be judged by the number of *conversions* we made. But that is exactly what we did.

Am I suggesting that God could not work through a legal clinic in an evangelistic way? Of course not. As Paul preached in Athens,

God sets the times and places for people's lives in order that they would encounter him, so I am comfortable seeing and celebrating the evangelistic fruit of any ministry initiative. No, the problem is more subtle than that.

One of evangelicalism's fatal flaws is that we usually frame justice as an expression of the Great Commission. Jesus sent us into the world to make disciples of all nations, and this disciple-making work requires a wide variety of strategies and approaches. Outreach ministry is our catchall designation for this collection of strategies. Unfortunately, many, or most, evangelical congregations categorize justice as outreach—work we do "out there." Seen as an application of the Great Commission, justice morphs into a strategy that helps us make disciples more efficiently. We wind up *doing justice so* we can win people to Jesus. On the face of it, it makes sense that justice would be framed this way. The problem is that framing justice as outreach is theologically inaccurate. The Scriptures do not frame the work of justice as a means to the end of evangelism. The commands to "loose the chains of injustice," to "break the yoke of bondage," and to see to it that widows, orphans, and immigrants flourish are rarely portrayed as a *missional* outreach strategy in that sense.

Framing justice as outreach is also practically problematic. In our normal ways of thinking about church ministry, we invite people to participate in outreach based on their personal preferences and passions. Folks passionate about youth ministry sign up for youth outreach. People fired up to serve others head to the park to distribute free water bottles. Evangelists head door-to-door to engage their neighbors in intentional spiritual conversations. There is something for everyone—in the work of making disciples everyone gets to play—and everyone gets to choose the outlet that suits them. When we frame justice as one of the options on the outreach menu of church life, church members sign up for opportunities to "do justice" by checking that box in the bulletin.

If justice is an option on the outreach menu, that means justice is optional for everyone. If you want to do justice, great! If not, we have other options better suited for you. A lot of churches operate this way, and it means we are shaping generations of Christians who feel free to opt in or out of the pursuit of God's shalom.

GREAT COMMANDMENT, NOT GREAT COMMISSION

Justice is not at home in the Great Commission, but it thrives in the Great Commandment. It is essential to our understanding of what it means to love God and love our neighbors, the commands by which our allegiance, obedience, and faithfulness to God will ultimately be evaluated. When we allow justice to become a mere outreach strategy, we fail to grasp this reality in two ways. First, if justice is made to serve the ends of outreach and evangelism, it is rendered impotent to deal with actual injustice experienced by neighbors God calls us to lovingly lay down our lives for. Splitting our focus in this way will mean justice takes a back seat to the more urgent "outreach" priorities. Second, justice as outreach fails to engage us in a formational way. If justice is always "out there" and its purpose is to "lead people to Jesus," it insulates us from the work God might want to do in our lives and in our congregation.[1]

Instead of compartmentalizing justice as outreach or evangelism, we need a fuller and more nuanced understanding of mission that sees God's intent as larger (though surely not less) than the salvation of souls. God is, in Christ, reconciling all things and renewing all of creation back to God's original intent. The story of what God is doing in the world through Jesus is bigger, better, and more beautiful than personal salvation, and we benefit from this enlarged view of God's salvific purposes. This worldview that sees the gospel of the kingdom of God as the ultimate renewal and restoration of all things gives shape to our understanding of the role of justice in the life of the church.

David Fitch contends that the vocation of the church is to embody "faithful presence" to God and neighbor in the world.[2] This is helpful language because it points us to the reality that the extent to which a church is faithfully present to God and neighbor in the world is the extent to which that church is participating in mission. This is the imaginative shift we need to employ to the work of justice as well. Justice must be more than an outreach strategy because it is both a matter of the character of our community (faithful) and our posture and practice in the world (presence).

Justice isn't an outreach strategy; it's a way of life for the people of God.

A WAY OF LIFE FOR THE PEOPLE OF GOD

The pursuit of justice is, first, about becoming a particular kind of people in the world. David Fitch is again helpful in noting that the pursuit of God's shalom requires a "new kind of formation." But rather than perpetuating discipleship and formation systems that focus primarily on individuals, we need to hear Fitch's call to see the church as a "social reality witnessing to God's kingdom in the world." Because of this, cultivating "faithful presence . . . must therefore be a communal reality before it can infect the world."[3] This is a critical reminder that the formation of a people, more than the formation of persons, is the baseline work of the church, including justice.

If we are to see new ways of pursuing justice in the world, we must see the work of extending God's shalom into the world inter- twined with becoming a just people ourselves. Overwhelmingly,

Scripture speaks of justice as a matter for the people of God, not to merely engage "out there" but to engage internally because the character of the people of God is measured by the extent to which they embody the justice of God in their way of life together.

This stresses the importance of cultivating a communal way of life—an ecclesiology that lives out the justice of God's kingdom. Cultivating an embodied way of life as a local church requires a dedication to communal discipleship that gives source and depth to the discipleship of individual believers. If justice is ever going to flourish in and through the local church, it will do so because evangelicals embrace the notion that becoming a just people is central to the formative work God wants to do in our midst. This is one reason why justice is so ill at home in evangelical churches. We have never really conceived of justice as an expression of faithful ecclesiology and formation.

MOVING AWAY FROM COMFY INDIVIDUALISM

There is a lie hidden in our belief that justice is but an option on the menu of church life, and it is wrapped up in our belief that we can live our lives inconsequentially. It seems we believe that our actions, choices, values, voting patterns, and so on do not impact people outside of our spheres of relationships. We have come to insulate ourselves from those who live outside our spheres and who experience the world in a manner much differently than we do.

That insulation works just like insulation is supposed to. It makes us comfortable. When I am cozily inside the warmth of my own home, I am unconcerned about the elements battering those who are walking on the sidewalk out front. The great tragedy of that way of life is that a comfortable life renders us indifferent to the discomfort of others. As Dorothy Day said, "People insulated by their own comfort lose sight of it." I no longer feel compelled to act with purpose and intentionality. It's not so much that I disagree with the notion that God intends everyone to experience shalom and flourishing but that I am warm and comfy where I am.

When Dr. King wrote his "Letter from a Birmingham Jail," he wrote it to pastors and religious leaders who could not see the world through the lens of his faith tradition. They were unable to understand the perspective of faith communities who were used to, and forced to, work out their faith "from below." So, when Dr. King asserts that "injustice anywhere is a threat to justice everywhere. We are caught in an inescapable network of mutuality, tied in a single garment of destiny. Whatever affects one directly, affects all indirectly," it would have been as obvious to him and his church as the notion that Jesus is Lord.[4] And yet this notion of a mutuality between oppressed and oppressor, between those on the margins and those onlookers from the sidelines, would have seemed foreign to the mainstream white audience Dr. King was attempting to reason with.

Melba Padilla Maggay, writing from her context in the Philippines, shares similar sentiments. "We live in the presence of one another. Human solidarity is such that we all suffer together. . . . Whether we like it or not, one person's deprivation is an indication of the guilt and humiliation of all."[5]

The notion that we somehow share in one another's reality because of our common humanity, and also because of our shared participation in a society with broken, unjust systems is nearly incomprehensible within the modern white evangelical imagination. American evangelicalism operates by an internal logic built on the primacy of the individual, and everything from our theological systems (think, penal substitutionary atonement) to our ministry strategies (think, four spiritual laws) is rooted in the foundational belief that faith is ultimately an individualist enterprise, a series of transactions between a human person and God.

A church full of people who are taught that faith is between them and God is perfectly positioned to assume that justice is not something that concerns them or their congregation. We can also fool ourselves into thinking that God's shalom is attained incrementally through the progress made possible by, say, hard work or good financial management. This makes an intentional pursuit of justice totally optional. Tragically, this approach to faith and the subsequent deprioritization of justice is precisely the kind of moderation that compelled Dr. King to write his letter from the jail in Birmingham in the first place.

The church suffers from a kind of atrophy of the muscles of shalom in the world. Maggay contends that our "inertia of indifference springs from the notion that we can live our inner lives with integrity without having to concern ourselves with the poor."[6] Sadly, to be a church who leaves the pursuit of shalom to others who are "more strategically positioned" reveals that we have fallen prey to the lie that we can live with integrity without a concern for the poor and marginalized neighbors in our midst.

My experience growing up and working within the white evangelical context has served to reinforce this observation. It is not something we left behind in the civil rights movement as though we had some great awakening with the passage of the Civil Rights Act of 1964. These are current problems. These are choices we are making today, choices that are shaped, informed, and codified through decades of indifference and generations of insulating ourselves from the injustice experienced by those at the margins of American society. This dynamic has accelerated the exodus of justice-seeking evangelicals from the daily life and ministry of the local church, folks who have opted to create alternative communities of support for the work of justice in the nonprofit and parachurch world.

Of course there is a fatal flaw in this plan. Despite the good work happening on the ground by those who find themselves at the margins of congregational life, this supposedly tidy division of duties is ultimately settling for something less than what God intends. God's intentions for shalom and justice will invite us to reconsider the divide and our way of being the church in the world.

GOD'S SHALOM IS EXPRESSED AND
EXTENDED IN THE PEOPLE OF GOD

God's shalom cannot be expressed fully (to the extent that we can experience it before the new Jerusalem) apart from the people of God embodied and rooted in local contexts. The reality of God's shalom (where nothing is missing and nothing is broken) is God's intention for all of creation. And that shalom is expressed in and extended out from a people in constant formation.

The formation of a people. God's shalom is most fully expressed to the world through the formation of a people. This is not to say that we don't, or can't, catch or create glimpses of God's intentions in other ways, but the 4K ultra HD picture of God's shalom is only available to be experienced in the context of a people.

God as the original expression of shalom. In the beginning, God. Before the creation of the world, before the destruction caused by sin, before the need ever arose for the work of justice, God.

And God is, in God's very essence, a people. It may seem a bit strange to say that God has existed throughout eternity in a peopled form, but central to what makes God, well, God, is that God exists in community. The Scriptures reveal this triune God to us as a community of three that make up the one true God of Abraham, Isaac, and Jacob.

That God has always existed in community is important because it is the baseline of our understanding of shalom. God, existing in perfection and harmony between Father, Son, and Spirit, is a communally embodied expression of shalom. In God nothing is missing and nothing is broken. In God there is no oppression or evil or injustice or marginalization. Each person of the Trinity exists in loving, dynamic mutuality with the other persons of the Trinity, and each in their specific way contributes to and submits to the community of the other. This community that God enjoys is the highest and greatest expression of God's shalom. It is this God-who-exists-as-shalom-community who then acts in the world in creation and re-creation.

Creation as the original extension of shalom. If, in fact, God exists in loving perfect union without need or want of any kind, what would motivate God to create?

This starts to make sense through the language of shalom. Shalom is *expressed* in a people and *extended* through a people. If that's the case, then God exists as the perfect *expression* of shalom, and creation serves as the original *extension* of shalom.

The reality of creation itself suggests that "it would not do" for God to stop at being simply an *expression* of shalom. Rather, God purposes to *extend* it out beyond the relational borders of God's shalom community. Shalom rightly expressed in community will *naturally* look to extend itself beyond its existing relational borders.

The creation narrative demonstrates God's work of extending the community of shalom beyond its initial boundaries. The physical creation becomes a tangible outworking of shalom, the Garden of Eden is, by existing, a metaphor of shalom. God is acting to create the conditions by which a larger number of persons might be able to participate in that community of shalom.

When God creates Adam and Eve, and by extension all of humanity, we witness a widening of the circle of persons who live within the relational borders of the shalom community. What was originally experienced in God by God alone is now an ever-widening circle of persons who participate in the community of God's shalom.

God's mandate to Adam and Eve aligns with this idea of expression and extension also. Adam and Eve become participants in the extension of shalom to the rest of creation. To care for the earth, to be fruitful and multiply, are tangible ways in which Adam and Eve demonstrate shalom community where nothing is missing and nothing is broken.

Sin and the shattering of shalom. The entrance of sin into the world fractures the shalom community. Within the *people of God* a fissure appears, brought on by the rejection of the dynamic, loving community of shalom in favor of a more individualized, self-centered existence. Tragically, sin not only shatters the capacity of humanity to *express* God's shalom, it undercuts our capacity to *extend* it as well. Within one generation we come to experience the gravest of injustices (murder) and a demonstrated inability to reclaim what was lost in the fall. In the earliest chapters of Genesis there is no room for what we have called *indifference* to God's shalom. Instead, there is only active rebellion against it. Shattering the shalom community results in a people who are now fundamentally unable to extend shalom and are hell-bent on breaking it down even further.

THE OLD TESTAMENT AND THE PEOPLE OF GOD

Given the reality of a shattered community of shalom in which the intentions of God are neither expressed nor extended, God launches a mission of redemption centered on a people. Surely there would have been infinitely better, more efficient, and more effective ways of addressing this problem. Instead, God opts to locate the mission in the midst of a people. This is what we see when God says to Abram that the people formed from his family will be both *blessed* and *a blessing to the world*. From the start, Israel was *formed* to be a people who both expressed and extended the shalom of God. What often becomes cliché in our church vision statements these days, this notion of "blessed to be a blessing" is, at its essence, something far more significant than random acts of kindness with a "Jesus loves you" sticker attached. It is a fundamental expression and admission that because the people of God uniquely bear witness to the intentions of God, the shalom of God will be expressed and extended through them. This isn't communicated in the form of a command (you *should* be a blessing). It is a straightforward articulation of reality. The shalom of God *will* extend through this people beyond their relational borders (transcending ethnicity, culture, religious practice, geography, etc.) because that's how shalom works.

Throughout the Israelites' journeys in the pages of the Old Testament, we see God reinforcing the notion that they are a people, and that they are God's people. In the people's liberation from Egypt, we see this clearly as God says, "I will take you as my own people, and I will be your God. Then you will know that I am the LORD your God, who brought you out from under the yoke of the Egyptians" (Exodus 6:7). God is pledging to do the very thing we observe in the creation narrative. There is an extension of shalom community to include a people outside the relational boundaries of the Trinity. Why does God do it this way? I'd argue shalom *can't not* work like this.

THE RE-FORMATION OF A PEOPLE

At the same time, this *people*, through whom the shalom community of God is expressed and extended, lives into that reality in fits and starts. This is why the expression and extension of God's shalom requires not only the consistent formation of a people but *also* the consistent *re-formation* of that very same people. This is why God gives us the prophets. This is a central point of the prophetic tradition throughout Scripture—reforming a people in and through whom the shalom of God might flow more freely and faithfully.

If God's shalom is expressed and extended to the world *through* God's people, then it is essential that we prioritize the cultivation of a particular way of life as a people. The character of our community is the foundation of both our faithfulness and our witness, our capacity to become a just people and our demonstration of God's justice in the world. To be about justice has to mean that we are also about the church—its formation and reformation.

From my view, though, the work of *forming and reforming* faith communities in the evangelical landscape has largely ignored the notion of God's community of shalom and has instead settled for a kind of *forming and reforming* around lesser visions, something less than church. It seems that we may have lost sight of the fact that the purpose of God's people in community is (literally *from the beginning*!) to be an expression and extension of God's shalom. To create forms of church in which justice and shalom are menu items for congregational life is to miss this point entirely. The work of justice is not optional and it's not outreach; it's a way of life for the people of God.

IMPLICATIONS FOR OUR LIFE TOGETHER

So, where do we begin? How might pastors and leaders lean into the work of developing an imagination for justice as a way of life?

To start, we will have to begin by reimagining formation and discipleship as a communal endeavor, and that begins with a radical commitment to a communal identity.

Our standard evangelical way of operating is to focus our efforts and resources on the development of individual believers. I affirm the need to disciple individual Christians well and deeply. But there is a difference between that and a capitulation to the individualistic idols of our culture. In the main, we have discipled people to believe that faith is nothing more than a personal relationship with God whereby I am saved, discover my individual identity, discern God's unique purpose for my life, and learn how my passions are things God gave me to, generally speaking, make the world a better place. Framed in the individualistic narrative of our society, the church then *can never be anything more* than a vendor of religious goods and services that distorts church life into a consumptive experience. When church operates in this manner, "the church becomes one more consumer-oriented organization, existing to encourage individual fulfillment rather than being a crucible to engender individual conversion into the Body."[7] As long as I am at the center of my religious experience, the church will function as a cosmetic appendage to my faith rather than a central way of being in the world. This devotion to a privatized, individualistic kind of faith is something distinctly white and Western. This pursuit is misguided and will ultimately keep us from cultivating communities of God's shalom.

The triune God gives us a picture of a purposeful community of mutual interdependence that seriously challenges any endeavor to understand ourselves or our relationship with God in any way outside of community. Jesus demonstrated this kind of awareness in the way he described his self-understanding related to his connection to the Father. Unless we learn to see ourselves as God does, as inextricably bound up with the lives of others in the shalom community of God, we will struggle to embody a communal way of life.

When we attempt to determine or understand our identity apart from others, we do so in a decidedly secular, nontrinitarian way. If we cannot know God apart from the reality of God in community within the Trinity, it stands to reason that as bearers of God's image we really can't know who we are apart from community as well.

ONCE YOU WERE NOT A PEOPLE

The communal identity of the church and the formational movement of God that is driving it are on display in 1 Peter 2:10: "Once you were not a people, but now you are the people of God." In just a single verse, Peter demonstrates the shift that must take place in the people who participate in our local congregational life. To experience life in the church requires a movement from "not a people" to "the people of God." The experience of Jesus' salvation includes shedding my individualism in favor of a new corporate identity. That means pastors need a vision for discipleship and formation that helps people shift from seeing themselves as autonomous individuals—an identity reinforced by nearly every other cultural message—to participants in a people.

One of the ways we tried to get at this when I was a pastor was to intentionally include the article *a* when we cast vision. So, we were not just *people following Jesus*, we were *a people following Jesus*. We discussed this change extensively, wrestling with whether people would even notice, and dealing with the fact that it was clunkier to say from the front on a Sunday. In the end, we decided to go with it and to embrace the *clunk* as the actual formational moment. We *wanted* people to trip on the language because it gave us the opening to do the identity formation we so badly needed and desired.

I often think though that we were probably working against ourselves because we didn't always do a great job with, say, the music we sang together corporately. Our go-to songs were still serving up a steady diet of *I* language that reinforced the individualist enterprise we were hoping to avoid. The goal wasn't to rid ourselves of the personal experience of God's grace, so I wouldn't have advocated for losing all the *I* language. But we didn't do a great job of thinking about balance and the consequences that even things like song choice had on the formation of *a people following Jesus.*

Consider the regular practices of your community . . .

- Is there more *I* or *We* language when you gather?

- How do you cast vision for participation in small groups, and does that language reinforce the idea that even small groups are primarily about individual benefit?

- What are you calling people to in your practice of the Lord's Supper: a personal encounter with Jesus or a communal sacrament for the people of God?

- What about baptism and baby dedications? Do we stop short in committing an individual to God, or do we remember the layer of marking that person for participation in a people?

We won't be able to make the shift overnight, but by recognizing the incredible power intentional language has over the culture of our communities, we can be making purposeful connections between the communal identity of God, the people of God in Scripture, and what it means to be the church today.

DISCERNING TOGETHER

We also have an opportunity to invite people into a culture of communal discernment instead of individual autonomy. Most pastors and leaders get a little antsy when thinking about the notion of discerning in community the issues facing a congregation. Many times this conjures images of antagonistic membership meetings and internal battles over the kind of coffee being served in the narthex. But most of these painful experiences come up because, instead of a truly communal identity, we come to decision-making as *individuals* concerned in the main *about personal self-interest*. This is the idol of self at work. We often fight because we have preferences that are not met. When those preferences are in jeopardy, I feel the right to assert *myself* and demand the entire community respond to my urges.

That is not what I'm talking about. Discerning together in community is a work of formation for the *people* who participate in *the people*. The first time I encountered this in ministry was on a Sunday morning when out of the blue one of the primary leaders in our church told me that their family was moving out of state—not for a new job or because of an unexpected crisis—just because. I guess that might sound like I disagreed with their decision, but I really didn't. I realized the decision bothered me not because of the decision but because it didn't square with my sense of how decisions like this get made. I had an expectation that this would be a decision processed among our leaders and within the congregation because that's what families do. I got mad because I got left out of the process. But—and this has taken a long time to come around on—the whole thing was my issue. As a church, we didn't have a communal identity. We weren't *we*; we were a collection of *I*'s. There was no reason for this family to submit this decision to the community because we weren't *a people*. And *that* formational work was mine to lead. What we missed here was not the chance to talk someone out of a major move. (I think it was a good move for them.) We missed the chance to celebrate it with them and to send them into what God might have next for them.

We need to lean into the work of cultivating communities where the notion of self is regularly put to death. This is work that starts with pastors and leaders within the church. Discerning together both the work of God in the church and in the lives of the leaders in the room, we begin to ask the question, *What seems good to us and the Holy Spirit here?* Not just once a year at the strategic planning retreat, but regular rhythms of laying our decisions out for the community to discern together. Inviting individuals to be open handed with self-interest creates a communal space where what God is saying and doing can be authentically discerned. If I truly can't know myself apart from my relations with others, then I can't authentically discern the will of God apart from that same community.

WHAT DOES THIS HAVE TO DO WITH JUSTICE?

If our goal is to cultivate a congregational way of life that authentically engages injustice toward the goal of God's shalom, we need to establish patterns and ways of thinking that help us resist turning the work of justice into an outreach strategy and relocates justice in the character of our shared way of life. But to do that we actually have to cultivate a shared way of life.

In my experience, forming a community that can seek the shalom of God in the world requires work that may not, at face value, look like "justice work." Yet it creates the conditions for justice to thrive. A serious commitment to communal identity and discernment helps to till the soil of our congregation so that the fruit of justice can establish deep roots.

Without a common sense of identity, it is nearly impossible to see our lives as bound up with the lives of others. Forming a community that helps people make the shift from *I* to *We* opens up a greater possibility that when we see injustice in the world, we will resist the temptation to view it from the vantage point of cozy individualism and instead have a way of *living out* the notion that we are bound up in a common humanity. Churches that have a vibrant sense of common identity intuit the shared experience of suffering where the afflictions of one affect the whole.

This also creates the space for discerning the times particularly related to injustice. If a church doesn't *already* have the DNA of communal discernment, it is a stretch to think that they could, for example, sit together and discern what to think about an issue as highly charged as community policing. To discern the movement of God in a community related to something like that, the groundwork has to already be in place.

Cultivating shalom communities is work that not only engages the *content* of justice but also the *practices, patterns, and values* required for a way of life together that gives faithful expression to God's shalom. This is how we become a people who can extend that shalom to the world.

QUESTIONS FOR CONSIDERATION

1. Take an inventory of ministry within your church you might categorize as justice. Catalog the language you use to motivate and cast vision for that work. Are you framing justice as a work of a people, or is it compartmentalized in outreach categories?

2. Many of us "do justice so that _____" (fill in the blank for your congregation). Why are you doing justice?

3. What might change about your congregational imagination for justice if the work shifted from outreach to a way of life? What changes would you as a leader need to make to help justice move from a Great Commission to a Great Commandment conversation?

4. Specific to your congregation, make note of the particular dynamics that might be working to resist justice? Think through pastoral approaches to moving beyond those roadblocks. What specific actions come to mind?

5. What factors might deepen the inertia of indifference for folks in your church? What steps can you take to lovingly push people outside of their comfortable spaces to consider issues of injustice?

6. Shaping a communal identity within a congregation is no small task. It might prove worthwhile to spend time as leaders discerning ways, large and small, of building this kind of identity into the DNA of your congregation. How do you move from people to a people?

2

EXILES IN THE
PROMISED LAND

THE CHURCH AS PROPHETIC ALTERNATIVE

What kind of people is required for justice to thrive? If justice as a way of life for a people is to gain traction in our life together, we have to point our life together in a particular direction. The shalom community of God has to have a distinctive character.

Would justice thrive in a congregation that functions as a mere affinity group? Probably not. As a pastor, I was always a little worried that this was as far as our congregational identity went—a group of people who came to the same room at the same time because we had some common convictions. Maybe that's not a bad start, but what's to keep people from a life of indiscriminate free association, choosing church based on a personal set of preferences that drives most of their other affiliations? Not much, I guess. Part of the pastoral task—shared among the community of leaders—is the work of moving affiliated persons into a deeply shared communal identity.

To live into an identity as the people of God, a new way is needed. An ecclesiology—not just theoretical or merely theological—but an embodied set of convictions shared in community about what it means to be God's people. This applied ecclesiology has to be able to create an imaginative identity where justice can flourish. This was one of the struggles in my first pastoral context. We had an openness for justice, but I didn't have a way to help us connect theology to practice—and we didn't have the ecclesial imagination—to sustain the hard work of justice. Our sense of justice as an outreach strategy, or as a way of showing kindness to neighbors, wasn't the set of broad shoulders we needed to hold up under the burden of the stresses caused by the work of justice. So, even though we were doing good ministry, we often fell prey to relational antagonisms that hampered the work's progression. There could have been countless reasons for that, but we were at least deficient in—if not downright starving for—an ecclesiological framework that could help us navigate the new world many of us were in.

So what kind of people ought we to be? Over the next three chapters, I want to develop this thought by looking at lenses that expand our sense of what it means to be a people and how justice might thrive in the midst of such a people.

CHURCH AS ALTERNATIVE COMMUNITY

The first move for any local church is to cultivate an imagination for church as an alternative community. That might seem basic, but we can't live into our call as God's people in the world unless we see ourselves as distinct from the world. In our distinction—our set apartness—we not only discern God's ways but our way of life in response. If, as Peter says, the church is "a chosen people, . . . God's special possession, . . . called . . . out of darkness into his wonderful light" (1 Peter 2:9), then we do well to embrace the serious otherness of our way of life in the world.

I've sometimes called myself an "armchair Anabaptist." I resonate deeply with the ethos of the Anabaptist and neo-Anabaptist movements—to the chagrin of some of my fellow justice practitioners.

More than likely conjuring images of remote enclaves of sequestered Christians (think Amish communities), Anabaptism seems to give them the impression of cult-like, cloistered, and altogether disengaged people, separate from the world and far from the critical work of justice. I've always contended that we ignore the contributions of Anabaptism in the work of justice to our detriment because Anabaptists have much to add to our understanding of church and the work of justice in the world—particularly in the area of ecclesiology. Anabaptism champions the idea of church as an alternative community, and while the temptation in developing this identity within the life of congregation could be cultural disengagement, it doesn't really have to be. On the other hand, living into and out of God's vision for his people in the world needs a deep corrective in many evangelical churches for which the Anabaptist vision of church as an alternative community does a lot of helpful work. So, go read *Resident Aliens*, and we'll pick back up when you're finished.

Now that you've digested all that, let's lay that framework of church as an alternative community over the work of justice. If a local church is to develop an alternative identity that is both distinct and engaged, we will have to cultivate an imagination capable of embracing the tension of otherness and engagement. We can do that by fleshing out our otherness through the language of exile.

CULTIVATING AN IMAGINATION FOR EXILE

In order to give the church an imagination for a way of life as God's people, Peter shapes their identity through the image of exile: "Dear friends, I urge you, as foreigners and exiles, to abstain from sinful desires, which wage war against your soul" (1 Peter 2:11). To be a people in exile is to be in a perpetual state of otherness.[1] And that experience of otherness is usually accompanied by a degree of hostility from the world. It's not just strange or sequestered otherness. Exiles live in the intersection of being both foreign and suspect.[2] Just think of the millions of refugees fleeing oppression, violence, and poverty. In nearly every case, these people are forced to live in a new place experiencing the hostility of others around them.

I suspect this is why Peter says that the church shares in the experience of Jesus of being simultaneously accepted by God but rejected by the world (1 Peter 2:4-5). The experience of exile means rejection. Of course, Peter is drawing on the exilic tradition of God's people. You can hear echoes of Jeremiah 29 in this passage from Peter. In Jeremiah 29, the prophet is proclaiming a message from God to a people in exile. They have been carried off to Babylon, a pagan city with no concern for their religious convictions and communal identity. It was ethnically, socially, economically, religiously *other*. Israel cannot hope to *integrate*; rather Jeremiah calls them to fashion their distinct way of life in Babylon. Jeremiah isn't worried about whether Babylon will eventually accept Israelites into the mainstream. The concern is the corporate character of the people being lived out in a place aggressively antagonistic to that way of life.

Peter is urging the church to cultivate an exilic identity that mirrors the experience of Israel in Babylon. The church is to cultivate a way of life distinct from the way of life that surrounds it. Stanley Hauerwas and Will Willimon say, "The church, as those called out by God, embodies a social alternative that the world cannot on its own terms know."[3] That is actually good news because it means we don't have to worry about being accepted into the mainstream of society. Like Israel in exile, and like Jesus himself, the more the church gives expression to the character of God, the more the church will be rejected by the surrounding

world. The church in exile sees its call as cultivating a particularly
kingdom-shaped way of life together in a culture that might be
aggressively antagonistic toward it.

This is what it means to say that the church is an *alternative
community* as opposed to seeing ourselves as merely countercultural.
We fall short when we content ourselves with the notion of church
as merely the development of a countercultural people. To be countercultural does not require the cultivation of an embodied alternative. A countercultural way of life *still accepts the inner logic of
society* as the starting point, in that, inherent to the language of
counter, we define ourselves by our contradistinctions. An alternative (exilic) community is forced to live out its *foreign* way of life
in the midst of a world that rejects it in a way that a counterculture
would not be required to. It does not define itself based on the
distinctions between it and the society it is embedded in. Rather,
it cultivates a way of life that is rooted *in some other place*.

CHURCH AS A PROPHETICALLY
ALTERNATIVE COMMUNITY

But that doesn't mean our way of life together has nothing to say
to the world we live in. In fact, the power of our witness against
injustice is magnified when we see our work as cultivating an alternative way in the midst of an old-way world. An authentically
alternative community—demonstrating the character and ethics of
the kingdom of God—is, in its otherness, functioning *prophetically*.

If, as Walter Brueggemann argues, "the task of prophetic ministry
is to nurture, nourish, and evoke a consciousness and perception alternative to the consciousness and perception of the dominant culture
around us," then we should see the role of the church similarly.[4] The
prophetically alternative community is nurturing, nourishing, and

evoking a way of seeing and being that stands in stark contrast to the world around us.

In 1 Peter 2:12, Peter demonstrates that the church, as an exilic people, will automatically have a way of life that functions as a prophetic alternative: "Live such good lives among the pagans that, though they accuse you of doing wrong, they may see your good deeds and glorify God on the day he visits us."

Recalling the creation narrative, and its role as the extension of God's shalom, Peter calls us to see the way of life of the church as *fundamentally good*. It is our work to live into and out of the shalom of God, the way any people called into the light and out of the dark would. Interestingly, this notion of a good way of life guards us against framing the prophetic character of our community as an antagonistic presence. The church is not called to lob our angry antagonisms this way and that. There are plenty of examples of how Christians across the theological and political spectrum settle for this manner of engagement. Understand this is not to say there is no time and place for genuinely faithful anger, but there is a difference between anger and antagonism, and cultivating a good way of life together helps us to resist the temptation toward antagonism.

And that good way of life is lived *among the pagans*. Exiles are forced to live in the midst of a dominant and oppressive foreign culture. There is an admission here that the way of life of the world is foreign to the kingdom of God (hence pagans), but also it is a confession that our life together is lived in the midst of that world.

We should expect that good way of life, lived among the pagans, *to draw their ire*. Peter reminds us that the good way of life of the people of God will collide with the sensibilities of society. There will be negative and aggressively antagonistic responses from the world to this way of life. Two things come out more clearly in this bit.

First, the world will *misunderstand* our way of life. The only way a fundamentally *good* way of life could be construed as fundamentally *wrong* is if that way of life stands in sharp contrast to the status quo (alternative) *and* is unintelligibly foreign to it as well (exilic).

Second, because this confusing way of life will elicit the *accusation* of wrongdoing, we can be sure that this *good way of life* will be viewed as an inherent *critique of the status quo.* If this good way of life did not function as an active critique of society, there would be no impetus for the accusation of wrongdoing. If this way of life was not by its nature a negative judgment of the way of life of the larger community, there would be no viscerally negative response. As Hauerwas and Willimon note, "people are crucified for following a way that runs counter to the prevailing direction of the culture."[5]

Too often this 1 Peter text feels underapplied to mean merely the cultivation of private morality, but private morality does not draw the ire of society. For a fundamentally good way of life to draw the ire of a culture, it must function in such a way as to publicly criticize the values and practices of the status quo and shine a light on the idolatries of a society.

But being prophetic cannot rely on merely articulating an opposition to injustice (though it's not less than that). Instead, the prophetic role of the church lies in the cultivation of an embodied witness against injustice. This public witness is animated by a way of life together. As Al Tizon says, "The church must stand apart from the world so that it can be faithful to its calling—namely, to be the conscience of the powers that be, as well as an alternative to a culture stained with idolatry, immorality, injustice and violence."[6] The church's way of life is fundamentally other, and by its very nature it holds a mirror up to the status quo of society, particularly in regard to injustice.

To faithfully critique the status quo of society we must dedicate ourselves to cultivating prophetically alternative communities of faith that embody our identity as exiles charged with living a foreign way of life in the world. This way of life must be robust and deep enough to bear the kind of fruit that is simultaneously *good* (shalom community) and prophetic enough to critique the idols of society.

This is critical because the idols of society are the doorways to injustice. We must reject the idols of America in our way of life together and do so in concrete ways in order that we might be accused of doing wrong, even as we are doing what is fundamentally good.

Consider, for example, the idol of American exceptionalism. American exceptionalism presumes a kind of omniscience and virtue that actively reframes the blighted history of our national story into a kind of heroic tale of the triumph of good. In part, this idol allows us to frame the notion of Manifest Destiny as a kind of divine right. Furthermore, that idol makes it possible to frame the annihilation and continuous systematic humiliation of indigenous peoples—until the present day—as an act of mercy for a "less-than-human people." There is a straight-line connection between this social idol and systemic injustice. It is but one example of the way in which social idols open the door to gross injustice.

AMERICA IS NOT THE PROMISED LAND

Sadly, the American evangelical church has largely rejected this notion of church as exilic community. Historically, we have tended to chafe against the idea of otherness and seek to escape experiences of cultural hostility. Instead of seeing ourselves as foreigners in a land of oppression (which is what a community in exile would always see clearly), we have labored to grasp for power and position in a land we conceive of as fundamentally good. To see society as fundamentally good, and to develop strategies of engagement that derive from that fundamental belief, is to reject our place as exiles.

If justice is to thrive in and through our shared life together, we will have to rid ourselves of our belief that the United States maintains favored-nation status with God or that somehow the United States is inherently virtuous. I don't mean we have to ignore the benefits of our system of government or reject everything American as evil. But the church that sees America as a Christian nation cannot also see itself as being in exile. The fundamental flaw in seeing the United States as fundamentally righteous (even if we get off track) is that injustice becomes an outlier experience in our nation. The role of the church in such a context would be the *formation* and *reformation* of this nation, and so it makes sense that so much evangelical consternation has been expended to try to get America to return to its Christian roots or to despair because of the reality of a nation that forgets God. This is not a problem only for the evangelical right. Many of the more progressive voices that have shaped Christian social engagement operate under the same fundamental assumption that the goal of the kingdom is the formation and reformation of a nation.[7] This perpetuates the false equivalence of America and the church, and fails to properly appreciate the definitive otherness called for by our true exilic identity. Seeing our call as the church and the work of justice as primarily reforming a nation-state is the fruit of our collective ecclesial identity confusion.

Instead of continuing to operate with a conflated national religious identity, we have an opportunity to embrace an identity of church as exilic community. This exilic community would always be aware of its fundamental and irrevocable otherness in the midst of a land that will ultimately reject it.

HOW DO WE RECOVER OUR PROPHETICALLY ALTERNATIVE IDENTITY?

There is no doubt this is going to require some work in our congregations. But there are some patterns we can establish within our life together that create some space to not only help our congregations live into our exilic otherness but to embrace the prophetic quality of that way of life.

If you've spent time pastoring in the local church, you've probably encountered the serious difficulty of approaching the topic of injustice in a congregation that isn't used to the conversation. In the white evangelical world, that is probably most of us. Issues of justice are like the third rail on a subway track—just don't touch it. Why do we have so much trouble? We can start to get at this question better when we look at it through the prophetic alternative lens.

We live in a world of partisan antagonism. In this world, justice issues always fall along the lines of partisan talking points. Even as you read this, you could probably create a list of justice issues and easily note which side of the partisan divide they fall on. The most critical issues of our day find their cultural source in the antagonistic battles of partisan politics.

Some of the biggest mistakes I've made as a pastor have been when I attempt to talk about justice issues without naming the partisan antagonisms that enslave us. When I acquiesce to the partisan cultural conversation around justice, I've given up the essence of what makes the church the prophetically alternative people of God. When I accept the premise of the question—the way American political culture wants to ask it—I become nothing more than a willing participant in the extension of these partisan antagonisms.

Tragically, this is the starting point for most evangelical congregations. We haven't narrated and embodied the ways of God in a manner that fully integrates the justice of God. In the absence of that kind of work happening in the church, people learn to frame justice issues from the dominant cultural narrative of partisan politics. We all have. The relative silence on justice issues over the decades within evangelicalism means that entire generations have grown up in the church without an imagination for any other way of framing justice issues.

So, if I stand up on a Sunday morning to speak about immigration or police brutality, the mental framework of folks in my congregation —the collective cultural DNA of our church—is significantly bent toward hearing my words through the lens of partisan antagonisms. I was preaching through Ephesians one time and, trying to give folks a mental image for the separation between Jew and Gentile in the temple courts, used the example of Jim Crow laws in the American South. Anecdotal at best, the reference came and went, and I was rather proud of myself for thinking of it. No sooner had I stepped off the platform on Sunday when I was angrily confronted about "bringing politics into the pulpit," and the antagonism continued well into the afternoon through a series of emails suggesting that my reference was an accusation that every member of the church was racist. To be honest, my first instinct was to get mad and take the critique personally or to dismiss it as evidence of someone who simply did not have ears to hear. But the more I reflect on this instance, and every other instance of this kind of thing—it's not uncommon, particularly in white evangelical spaces—it was simply evidence of being enmeshed in a partisan worldview. We *started* our understanding of justice enmeshed with partisan antagonisms, and my mention of injustice triggered an unhealthy exchange of antagonisms.

So, am I saying don't preach or engage justice issues in corporate gatherings? Not at all. But it would probably save us some headaches if we tempered our expectations about what this accomplishes on its own. It might feel cathartic to get something off our chest, but unless our preaching on injustice is matched or exceeded by off-line work that tills the soil, it seems that preaching alone will be ineffectual.

We need a way of renarrating justice that resists devolving into the partisan antagonisms, and it's pretty hard to do that on Sunday morning. I've found that people need spaces not just to be talked to but to discern together the way the Scriptures intersect with the issues of our day. These spaces have to go beyond the standard didactic classroom environment. People have to engage in the process of discernment. But we have to do this in community. Without the overarching sense that we are reaching for a communal identity out of which we understand what it means to be the church, we stand to reinforce our individualist impulses. These spaces are critical because we are inviting people into an experience where they will confront the narratives they use to interpret the world. This is inherently destabilizing. Pastorally, there's a responsibility to shepherd people in the midst of that destabilizing work. This isn't caving to the fragility in the congregation. It's stewarding the lives of people God has given us to care for.

Once we create these spaces, we are aiming to pull out of the partisan antagonisms and see issues of justice through the lens of God's kingdom. Paul's admonition to the Ephesians is instructive for us: "Our struggle is not against flesh and blood, but against the rulers, against the authorities, against the powers of this dark world and against the spiritual forces of evil in the heavenly realms" (Ephesians 6:12). Overcoming the partisan antagonism means relocating the conversation. Paul reminds us that the entire struggle of good and evil is a cosmic battle. Justice is not a partisan endeavor, it is supremely spiritual in nature. Partisan politics is a "flesh and blood" struggle. When we concede to the partisan whims of our culture, we reduce God's justice to an issue of flesh and blood. Stepping back from the twenty-four-hour news cycle to consider injustice from God's perspective helps us imagine our way of life as distinct from the political left or right. Creating the space to dwell in the text together in the company of God's Spirit opens a path to seeing the alternative way of God take shape.

People need to be able to connect concrete issues to the spiritual battle of Ephesians 6. The battle Paul talks about isn't just the battle of personal sin but all the ways the enemy corrupts our capacity to experience life as God intended. Injustice is tangible evidence of the kingdom of darkness at work in the world. Committing ourselves to this kind of conversation helps us—collectively—to resist the partisan antagonisms all around us.

The danger here is that this might feel like permission to view injustice as merely spiritual. If we left our conversations in the vaguely spiritual realm, we would fall prey to the #thoughtsand prayers problem of seeing the solution to injustice as something less than concrete in the everyday experience of people living under broken systems. *Nothing we can do. Our battle isn't a human one, it's a spiritual one.* It is, frankly, something to consider since evangelicals have a tendency to spiritualize concrete realities into vagaries and abstraction. But it doesn't have to be this way. In fact, seeing injustice through this supernatural lens *can* actually help us bring it back to the ground and land it in a new space. Part of the work of pastoral leadership is honing the capacity to help folks *commute* between the reality of the spiritual battle and the fact that this spiritual battle expresses itself through concrete examples of oppression, marginal-ization, and injustice. These concrete realities are expressions of sin and the power of the enemy prowling around like a roaring lion.

Learning to renarrate the existence of injustice and to relocate it outside of partisan politics is essential because when injustice is an expression of the power of the enemy it means we are free to stand against it. It means we can't be indifferent or agree to disagree. Racism is sin, and we can say so. The mistreatment of immigrants and refugees is an affront to God, and we can align together in that accord. Codified inequity in the education of kids living in poverty is an egregious defamation of the *imago Dei*, and we do not have to resort to political antagonisms to make such an argument.

If our congregational conversation about injustice is partisan, the best many of us can hope for is a kind of mediated detente. But since injustice isn't merely a flesh-and-blood battle (people aren't the enemy after all), and it is evidence of the cosmic battle of the kingdom of God and the kingdom of the enemy, then we are free—required even—to stand against the devil's schemes. It's not partisan arguing, it's resisting and rejecting the powers and principalities.

But this is a work we need to do together, in community, involving people in the work of discerning, surrendering, and realigning, and where we learn the difference between the things we can agree to disagree on and the things we must categorically reject as his people. Without this work, it all gets lumped together along partisan fault lines.

If the enemy is the father of lies, then we can see these spaces as learning to name and reject the lies that have taken root in the world. Perhaps there is no better example of this than the lie of racial difference. There is no way to suggest that racism is open for difference of opinion within the church. It is a lie from the enemy that can and should be resisted and rejected when we see it. And yet even something as fundamental as the inherent dignity of persons created in the image of God is up for debate in congregations that haven't done the work of renarrating and relocating their engagement with injustice.

Upon reflection, I've noticed a pattern in my pastoral life. These spaces of participatory, communal discernment on issues of justice are something I've entered with a decent degree of frequency. (We would meet weekly to discuss theological and cultural justice-related issues.) These regular gatherings included a mixture of teaching, discussion, reflection, prayer, and application. Our goal was to help us—together—make connections between Scripture and the world. These are spaces that engage a people in work we do all the time in all kinds of ways, but toward the end of justice and God's shalom. Without exception, people who come to those spaces and participate in a communal process are able to form new patterns related to injustice. These folks are personally able to renarrate issues through the lens of the kingdom of God and are able to resist partisan antagonisms. I have never gotten angry pushback from someone who came to these spaces. Ever.

It's an ongoing process for all of us. None of us learn in a short time how to resist the partisan world we live in and might even drift back over time if we stop prioritizing these kinds of spaces. But that ongoing process is evidence of just how critical it is for us to create patterns of communal participation in the work of discerning the otherness of our exilic way of life in an unjust world. The tough personal work for pastors in these contexts is to receive pushback for what it is, evidence of a person who is drowning in an ocean of partisan antagonism. Imagine the possibilities for a congregation where angry partisan fighting only served to deepen the pastoral impulses of its leaders as they look at a people who are tossed about by the banal utterances of cable news.

The goal of creating these spaces is not just to settle what we think about a particular topic. That reinforces the temptation many of us have to assume that knowing the right things counts as living faithfully. So we create spaces not to merely think right but to discern *the right*. What is the lie in the world? What has God to say about the lie? Our calling as God's people is to *embody* an alternative to the world. The alternative to the lie is the truth. The alternative to evil is good. The alternative to ugliness is beauty. Congregational life comes alive when we commit to regular rhythms of discerning the true, good, and beautiful life we are called to live in the world. It's how we *live such good lives among the pagans* and how that life serves to critique the status quo of an unjust world.

We are called to be a people. But not just any people or a group of people joining a club centered on Jesus. We are called to be a people who cultivate an alternative way of life in the world. This way of life will be other to the world around us. In its purest form we can be sure it will be rejected, even angrily, because the good way of life we are growing together serves to critique the normal operating procedure of society. As a people in exile, we are called to cultivate a way of life that reflects the values and ethics of someplace foreign to a world marked by oppression and injustice. This foreign way of life will bear a distinctive kind of fruit: the fruit of God's intentions.

QUESTIONS FOR CONSIDERATION

1. Alternative community can be a strange concept. What adjustments can be made to your approach to ministry that can help people understand and embrace the notion of an alternative community?

2. Living as exiles might feel depressing to your people or opposed to some long-held beliefs about the role of church in society. Getting our identity right leads to freedom, though. If you were to outline a strategy for helping people resist

cultural assimilation—without becoming a cult—and to also develop a way of life that critiques the unjust systems and structures of our society, what small steps would you take initially? Six months from now, what would you want to see in your congregation?

3. Evangelicalism grew up in a kind of cultural exile, fighting so-called culture wars and cloistered from society. This is fundamentally *not* what the prophetically alternative church looks like when it seeks God's shalom. But there is a fine line. Within your congregation there will likely be a point of conversation about maintaining the distinctive otherness of a people in exile without losing the capacity to critique the status quo of society at the same time. Your leadership team should think through the particulars of how you seek to engage the world to stand against injustice without devolving into either an antagonistic or isolated community.

4. What rhythms already exist in your church that could be adapted to create space for building a community of discernment related to justice?

5. Where do you sense your congregation, or individual folks, falling into the pattern of partisan antagonisms? What windows of opportunity exist for reframing the conversation?

3

DEMONSTRATING
MAÑANA

THE CHURCH AS A PARABLE OF GOD'S INTENT

Bay Ridge, Brooklyn, was almost like a land before time. Cut off from the rest of the borough by the Gowanus Expressway, it escaped much of the rapid transformation of the city. In the time that I lived and pastored there, it still had the feel of a stereotypical 1950s–1970s New York film—think *Saturday Night Fever*—a gangster movie with over-the-top characters and outrageous accents.

But all wasn't as it had been. Historically an Italian, Irish, and Scandinavian enclave, the twenty years prior to my arrival saw an influx of new immigrant groups that, while not completely over-turning the cultural trappings of the neighborhood, had significantly altered life in the neighborhood and surrounding communities. My first urban living experience was overflowing with cultural expressions from all over the world: China, Jordan, Egypt, Syria, Yemen, Mexico, Russia, Albania. The list was as long as there were city blocks to explore. We loved being thrust into an immersive cultural experience, and the collision of ethnic groups meant—coming from the outside into the middle of it—we could explore these cultures easily and with great intentionality.

Not everyone shared my wide-eyed enthusiasm though. The in-coming ethnic groups represented change to long-standing tradition and culturally sequestered ways of life, and the demographic shift only slightly preceded a decline in some of the more revered traditions in the community. To be white (including the ethnically Old World Europeans) in Bay Ridge was to be a minority in a community that had been "yours" just two decades earlier. I suppose I shouldn't have been surprised then by the regularity and veracity of the racial unrest I experienced there, but I was. I was caught off-guard by the way white folks derisively renamed Bay Ridge "Beirut." It took me aback to hear neighbors talk about the flippin' camel jockeys (they didn't say flippin'). I didn't expect the widespread leaflet campaign that inundated the neighborhood demanding people not sell their houses to Chinese families. I didn't know what to do the day I walked across confetti-like slips of paper covering the sidewalk exclaiming "Kill the Jews." These experiences were normal in our neighborhood. What felt initially like an aberration became a reflection of the racist attitudes of the white community in our supposedly sleepy corner of New York City. I got used to the casual racialized language that peppered people's speech, and to being stopped in the street by a white person—because I was the only other white person around—asking me, "Can you believe all this?" with a dismissive head nod to the diversity moving around us.

This was the place I was called to be a pastor and the place we were called to be God's people. I became obsessed with the question of what the church might have to say in such a community. What does the gospel have to do with this? The way we answered these questions would determine the character of our witness in the neighborhood.

Of course, we understood that as the church we were called to be the salt of the earth and the light of the world. In a community where racial hatred churned under the surface, it was easy to see our community as an alternative to that. But we would need something more. At least that's what I learned along the way and after the fact. It was easy enough to know that we were called to be a different kind of community from what we saw all around us. But if the essence of the prophetically alternative community is embodying what is true, good, and beautiful in the face of what is untrue, evil, and ugly, then we couldn't afford to misconstrue *prophetic alternative* for mere *antagonism* or *countercultural* critique. We would need to see our way of life as an embodied witness *toward* something, not just *against* something. We would have to let our true, good, and beautiful way of life offer the compelling alternative that critiqued the injustice we saw all around us. We would need to see our life together as a parable.

CHURCH AS PARABLE

Understanding how Jesus used parables helps us understand how the idea of a parable can serve as a way of life for the church. Perhaps no other writer has shaped my understanding of parables more than Eugene Peterson in his book *The Contemplative Pastor*.[1]

> Jesus' favorite speech form, the parable, was subversive. Parables sound absolutely ordinary: casual stories about soil and seeds, bandits and victims, farmers and merchants. And they are wholly secular. . . . As people heard Jesus tell these stories, they saw at once that they weren't about God, so there was nothing in them threatening their own sovereignty. They relaxed their defenses. They walked away perplexed, wondering what they meant, the stories lodged in their imagination. And then, like a time bomb, they would explode in their unprotected hearts. An abyss opened up at their very feet. He was talking about God; they had been invaded!

If the church is a parable, that means it's going to be an ordinary yet subversive force in the world. Church-as-parable communities are able to integrate into the ordinariness of everyday life. At face value there is nothing decidedly other about them, and this ordinariness keeps the world from being on edge. The world does not feel its sovereignty threatened. But there is something about our way of life that will, upon reflection, begin to seem peculiar. As the world receives the church, it is unknowingly welcoming a subversive community into its midst, a community it will no longer be able to shield itself from because it has become part and parcel of its shared life. That peculiar way of life that seemed ordinary is really anything but. The great chasm of God's redemptive mission opens up at the feet of those who have relaxed their defenses as they see—maybe clearly for the first time—what a true, good, and beautiful life actually looks like.

This was a large part of the work of being the church in Bay Ridge. Our physical building was located at the center of these colliding ethnic groups. Like the hub of a bike tire with spokes radiating out from the center, we could look in any direction and see the effects of immigration patterns on our community. Within our collection of congregations under one roof, we represented nearly all the ethnic groups that resided in our larger neighborhood. That meant that we had an opportunity. We had an opportunity to do more than simply advertise that we could provide ministry for any family in the neighborhood. It meant that we could cultivate an alternative way of life that put God's intentions on display. In our serious wrestling with how to be God's people together and the struggles we faced in the day-to-day ministry together in such a diverse community, we could put a way of life on display that challenged the racism of our community constructively. Instead of merely rejecting what we were against, we could put flesh on our critique by living the good way of life among the pagans that God would call us to.

This was easier said than done. It exposed a lot in us that we probably wished we could have kept closed off. I know it did in me. But the more we labored in this work the more fruit we saw. The *character* of our life together was bearing witness to the world. When we celebrated the opening of our immigrant legal center, local politicians got a taste of the kind of community God would find familiar. These folks from "outside" found themselves in a living, breathing parable of the kingdom. When a local church takes seriously this call to *parabolically* embody the intentions of God, it means that the church is now able to both meaningfully engage its community and demonstrate the serious challenge of the kingdom to the status quo.

Our church was the Revelation 7 future of God showing up in twenty-first-century New York City. You could understand a bit of what God might be up to in the world by being part of this community of faith. This is true for every church. As a prophetically alternative people, we enact a parable of God's future. This means the church is profoundly eschatological.

The work of justice depends on a deeply eschatological church because the story of God's kingdom is the only story compelling enough to topple an empire. It is the only future reality that silences the oppressor and looses the chains of injustice. No other story can bear up under the weight of injustice and oppression, let alone enact a new kind of world in which that injustice crumbles in ultimate defeat. To live out of any other story is to live out of a story doomed to disappoint. To allow another story to animate our way of life together is to concede that we will fail to express and extend God's shalom as fully and faithfully as we could.

We are a people of God's tomorrow, today.

MAÑANA

In his book *Mañana: Theology from a Hispanic Perspective*, Justo González writes that the Christian life "is life lived out of an expectation, out of a hope and a goal. And that goal is the coming reign of God."[2] González frames the church as a kind of *mañana* people, a people who live out the character of God's tomorrow today. Something about the future reality of God's kingdom shapes our present day with a unique character.

What will tomorrow bring? González says, "Mañana is much more than 'tomorrow.' It is the radical questioning of today. . . . The real mañana is a time unlike today. It is a time of a new reality."[3] If the church is to embody the future intentions of God in the midst of the present day, it serves us to ask, What will tomorrow be like? What do we know of God's tomorrow that will allow us to give expression to those intentions today? Questions like these shine light on the reality that eschatological realities are not pie-in-the-sky considerations. Understanding and discerning the ultimate telos of the story of what God is doing in the world through Christ is serious work that has significant ramifications for the work of justice.

Earlier we considered the reality that God's initial intentions in creation were the expression and extension of shalom through expanding the number of those who participated in the shalom community of God. In the fall, that intent is hampered through the rejection of that shalom community by humanity. Jesus represents the fullest expression of God's mission to not just restore shalom but to restore the original shalom community. So if we were to hypothesize about the ultimate intentions of God, it would make sense that the story ends in a final recovery of this original design. We ought to be able to see the imagery of the shalom community of God being expressed and taking root throughout the whole created order. We would expect to find evidence of a people gathered in dynamic relationship with one another and with God, the community therein marked by total shalom and flourishing.

Throughout the pages of Revelation, this is exactly what we find. In Revelation 7:9-10 there is a people gathered from every tribe, tongue, and nation. This is evidence of the restoration of shalom in that these are the fault lines of shattered shalom as well. In Revelation 21 we encounter a new heaven and new earth, renewed in fact—a restoration of God's intention—where shalom is fully expressed and has indeed extended to all of creation. The evidence of this is that the fruit of sin and death are done away with. Similarly, Revelation 22 gives us a picture of a whole creation restoration, where nothing is missing and nothing is broken. In Revelation 21–22 the surest sign of this total restoration is a people gathered together with God at the center of this shalom community. In echoes of the promise to Abram, where this notion of a people takes concrete shape in the people of Israel, in Revelation 21:3 we hear a voice proclaiming that the intentions of God have finally reached their ultimate telos of a dynamic, expansive shalom community, saying, "Look! God's dwelling place is now among the people, and he will dwell with them. They will be his people, and God himself will be with them and be their God."

God's tomorrow is an eternal shalom community where everything wrong has been made right. These are the intentions the church is called to reveal in the world "as long as it is called 'Today'" (Hebrews 3:13).

And that means that God's tomorrow fills today with unshakable *hope*. The experience of the world today, particularly for those who experience that world at the margins of society, is marked by discouragement, struggle, pain, and injustice. In light of that lived reality, animating our life together through the lens of God's to-morrow creates a way of enduring and even thriving in the face of a harsh reality.[4]

But God's tomorrow also shines a light on the brokenness of the present. God's tomorrow functions as a "word of judgment on today."[5] Because God's tomorrow includes the complete restoration and renewal of all things, that future reality exposes the ways in which our world is yet to be restored and renewed. The corruption of God's original creative intent is seen for what it is, something less than the sweeter song of God's new creation.

Mañana is the modus operandi for the church, a way of being in the world. To see the church as a *mañana people* means we envision a community that embodies the tomorrow of God in this present age. The eschatological reality of God's kingdom is not a force pulling us into a sleepy kind of presence in the world, content to sing the songs of the "sweet by and by" while the world goes to hell in a handbasket. Instead, it breathes life into the soul of the people of God. God's tomorrow gives us vision, motivation, and resilience in the cultivation of the peculiar way of life for God's people.

Mañana is essential to the work of justice. González argues that *mañana* makes a new form of social action possible,

> one that seeks not merely the evolution of today into tomorrow but rather the breach that *mañana* announces. This is the practice of the prophets. This is also the manner in which the early church is politically active. It is a small group of insignificant people, and yet their activity soon brings upon them the wrath of the mighty Roman empire. Why? Because by their mere existence, by their living out of *mañana*, they question the very foundations of the Roman social order.[6]

By their living out of mañana, they question the very foundations of the social order. If this is true, it must change the way we understand our pursuit of justice in the world. It invites us to see our way of life as the embodiment of God's tomorrow, and that in doing so the shalom of God is expressed and extended to the world.

What does it look like to embody those intentions? Tangibly, what does it look like to be a *mañana* people? It is not a totally foreign notion that the church is a community where God's intentions are lived out, but it is worth making a few observations about the character of that life.

First, embodying the intentions of God is not an incrementalist approach to the spread of the kingdom of God. Several theological streams—and justice advocates—promote the notion that the church is active in the spread of the kingdom tangibly on earth. Churches often speak of "taking kingdom ground" or use other language that evidences a belief in the notion that our work on earth has a constructive quality, meaning, we actually *expand* God's kingdom through our work. Ultimately, we are talking about a way of seeing the role of the church and a way of framing the eschatological reality (God's tomorrow) as something that will *eventually* come into being through the faithful labor of the church. However, recalling González, this is a notion we do well to resist. Of our work in the world, he says it "seeks not merely the evolution of today into tomorrow but rather the breach that mañana announces." The church is not creating God's tomorrow today, but rather revealing or proclaiming that God's tomorrow has already broken into today in the person of Jesus. The incremental notion of the spread of God's kingdom does not seem to take seriously enough the eschatological proclamation of Jesus that the kingdom of God has drawn near in him; nor is it supported by the scriptural evidence that seems to suggest that in the return of Christ the established kingdom takes its final form.

This could seem to contradict the notion that the church gives expression to *and extends* God's shalom in the world. But the church isn't establishing the kingdom. It's embodying an eschatological reality. Hauerwas and Willimon argue that

> the political task of Christians is to be the church rather than transform the world. One reason why it is not enough to say that our first task is to make the world better is that we Christians have no other means of accurately understanding the world and rightly interpreting the world except by way of the church. Big words like peace and justice, slogans the church adopts under the presumption that, even if people do not know what "Jesus Christ is Lord" means, they will know what peace and justice mean, are words awaiting content. The church really does not know what these words mean apart from the life and death of Jesus of Nazareth.[7]

It is true that the church both expresses and extends the shalom of God into the world, but these dynamics are set in motion in Jesus. The church is not responsible for the extension of God's shalom in a way that relies on us to incrementally bring it into existence. Rather, the church is a people who embody the eschatological reality that in Christ the shalom community of God has been and is being restored. This is not to say that people who find themselves on the outside looking in are unable to experience and even become participants in the shalom community. On the contrary, this is one of the primary ways the shalom of God is extended when we embrace our role to be the people of God through whom God's shalom is revealed and will flow toward its intended transformative end.

DEMONSTRATION PLOTS OF THE KINGDOM

This tension is held together well in the agricultural metaphor of demonstration plots. A demonstration plot is a small, sequestered section of a farmer's acreage set aside for experimenting with innovative seeding or cultivation methods. It's called a "demonstration plot" because its purpose is to show others what these new ways produce. Other farmers can observe these alternative methods in action and judge for themselves if this is a direction worth traveling themselves. The demonstration plot doesn't take new ground itself, rather the acres around it change *only insofar as the demonstration plot reveals an alternative way compelling enough to be embraced by others.*

Similarly, the church is a demonstration plot of the alternative way of being a people in the world. Embodying God's tomorrow—today—is an ongoing act of demonstration. Local churches are communities set aside for putting a different way of life on display for a watching world to observe. Again, Tizon is helpful here, arguing that by "being the church, we present an inherent invitation to onlookers that says something like, 'do you like what you see? Come and join us.'"[8] This is the demonstration plot at work. Because we are primarily responsible for our way of being, the church is not responsible for taking new ground (the incrementalist approach) but rather with giving authentic expression to God's intentions and finding ways of extending that way of life out into the world such that the community witnesses the possibilities of the shalom community of God. As we "go out into the world" we do not go as people establishing the kingdom through our work even though, paradoxically, our life together does "extend God's goodness to the ends of the earth."[9] Our way of life together, in and through the church, is a revelation and demonstration of God's intentions.

What this will reveal in us. If we take seriously our call to be a demonstration of God's tomorrow, it will first expose ways in which we ourselves are out of alignment with God's intentions. For example, we should expect this kind of growing theological imagination to reveal the extent of our own obsession with cultural relevance.

There is a deep incongruence with being a people embodying God's tomorrow and *obsessing over fitting in with the cultural "today."* Perhaps nothing demonstrates our lack of theological imagination regarding the church in this way more than our obsession with relevance. Lesslie Newbigin writes that "a church which is merely trying to keep up-to-date is much more pathetic and ridiculous than a church which is merely clinging to the past. Not every new fashion . . . is the work of the Holy Spirit."[10] Obsessing over ways we might demonstrate our cultural relevance can distract us from the real work of being a church that demonstrates God's tomorrow today. It is evidence of a stunted understanding of the exilic and alternative nature of the church too. It's not to say that churches should *try to* be lame and out of touch, or that there isn't a place for cultural forms that are simple and fun, or that churches shouldn't work to appreciate God's common grace and celebrate the ways in which culture provides ways of delighting in the world. But this is not the key to unlocking the mission of God.

A great chasm of difference exists in my mind between *relevance* and *ordinariness*. Certainly, both come with a degree of welcome from society, but they are sourced out of different desires. On the one hand, ordinariness is a definitively human work. It celebrates the shared experiences of our humanity and the creative and collaborative potential in communities between friends and neighbors. It looks to participate in meaningful ways in the human enterprise of creating, tending, and celebrating the world well. Focusing on ordinariness will serve to help a church connect and engage the actual place they live and the actual people who share that space with them. This kind of church will dig deeper into a community, connecting in creative ways that help them know the names, stories, and desires of their new friends and long-time neighbors.

Relevance—which I distinguish from the critical value of contextualization—is fundamentally imitative (rather than creative). Relevance doesn't create, it mimics. It appropriates the superficial forms and sensibilities of the larger culture. The quest for this superficial expression of relevance is a quest to be accepted by society on society's terms. When churches settle for trying to imitate the culture of our society, it reveals a loss of focus on the cultivation of God's tomorrow and the call to cultivate a prophetically alternative community. Rather than understanding the real nature of church as parable, an obsession with relevance turns the church into a kind of superficial bait-and-switch where the "Jesus rabbit" is pulled out of the relevantly styled hat, sadly, in expected and cheesy ways. The reality is that a church is never going to be accepted by society. Society cares nothing for the essential commitments of people of faith, and so the notion that the only thing stopping us from meaningful revival is a relevant veneer to the message is naive to the core.

Recently, I ran across an article from *Vice* titled "Meet the Young Woke People Trying to Make Christianity Cool Again," which was celebrated on my social media feeds as positive progress for the church.[11] The article detailed the way that young, justice-minded leaders were producing an expression of Christianity that was appealing to the more progressive culture, a culture that has historically rejected faith as out of touch or worse. To me, this is a crystal-clear example of the way our quest for relevance corrupts our capacity to see church as a parable of God's intentions. If we employ the work of justice/shalom toward the end of cultural acceptance, we have essentially equated God's shalom with what are usually progressive cultural proclivities. Not only is this shoddy theologically speaking, it also robs us of our capacity to be an authentic people of God's tomorrow. Relevance, or the cultural recognition of being "woke" or "with it" is not really the goal, is it?

This is not to say that we will never find common ground with our culture. Of course, we will discover—because of our common humanity—that we will enthusiastically be able to collaborate with people outside the church.[12] However, accepting the assumptions of our culture for fear of losing relevance is a recipe for unfaithfulness. It is a question of the order of operations. To capitulate to the pressure to be relevant means that I am allowing the cultural *today* to inform my understanding of God's *tomorrow*. This is, of course, the exact opposite of the movement the church is called to. If the reality of God's tomorrow is the definitive lens through which we discern the cultural moment called "today," then we cannot begin that discernment under pressure to conform to the culture all around us.

It is exceedingly good news for us that committing ourselves to cultivating embodied expressions of God's tomorrow reveals the way we have come to obsess over being culturally relevant. Rather than functioning like society's dorky little brother, pleading for it to *please just call us cool*, we can reject that entire endeavor in favor of saying our role is cultivating something wholly other (rather than relevance). Our calling is not to mimic the same old way things have always been done but to be a demonstration plot of the ways of God in a world that knows nothing of the sort. To enact a living parable of God's tomorrow in the midst of today.

ON EARTH AS IT IS IN HEAVEN

Perhaps my favorite show of all time is *This Old House*. If you've ever watched the show you know that it is usually an extravagant restoration of a historic home for a young, well-resourced family. However, over the past few years this has not always been the case. One season captured my imagination in a way that has deeply informed my view of what it means to be the church. This season featured the story of a home restoration in the historic Roxbury neighborhood of Boston, one of the oldest neighborhoods in one of the oldest cities in the nation. Like many neighborhoods of similar origin, Roxbury played a significant and storied role in the early formation of the nation, and it has a rich history full of rich tradition and meaning. Also similar to neighborhoods in central cities, over time Roxbury has fallen into disrepair, complete with the requisite amount of blight, crime, and white and wealthy flight to "safe" places. As a result, the neighborhood came to represent a kind of regret that something once so grand could have fallen so far.

The house restored was an example of this decay. Centuries old and full of history, this house had become blighted and abandoned. Over a few months' time, the crew worked tirelessly. This project was the first to feature the twenty-four-hour camera set up to monitor the progress. As the crew wrapped up the Roxbury house, they showed the time lapse video of the entire project. It was amazing to watch. At no point of that video did the house move at all. Its structure was always entirely intact. The workers scaled its roof and worked up, down, and around until it was restored to an amazingly beautiful state. Gone was the blight, and now a young, working-class family was moving in to enjoy it. Incredibly, at the end of the video, they said that 95 percent of the house had been replaced. Of that entire structure, only 5 percent of the original house remained, which, in the process of transformation, seemed to never move an inch.

So . . . was it the same house? There's no way you could say no to that. We watched the house stay there the whole time. But was it a new house? With only 5 percent of the original material remaining, you'd have to say yes, right? It was the same and it was new. It was authentically renewed. Eschatologically speaking, this is the telos of creation, right? For Jesus to declare in Revelation 21 that "I am making everything new!" means that there is a definitive quality of newness to the ultimate experience of the shalom of God. But at the same time Jesus doesn't say "I am making all new things." So it's still the same old creation with a definitive renewal. This Roxbury house is a parable of new creation.

So too was its effect in the neighborhood. At the wrap party, they mentioned that as a result of the *This Old House* project, neighbors up and down the street had embarked on renewal and renovation projects of their own, and had opted into a community-wide movement of restoration and renewal such that the individual house transformation was now beginning to extend beyond itself to others. The house itself became a demonstration plot of the possibility of transformation, and those who came to observe bought into the vision for themselves. The work of restoring the home in a blighted community was prophetic because it dared to challenge the status quo of society that had all but written off the neighborhood for greener pastures. That work also served as a parable of God's intentions for humanity in a way that invited the people to join in with it.

I often imagine that this isn't happening on a network television show. I imagine that the WGBH Boston production team isn't at the center of this project, but locally rooted shalom communities of God are. I imagine embodied faith communities who see the work of transformation of people and place not as a mechanism of "bringing the kingdom" but rather as a declarative signpost that God intends to make everything right and new again. They see God restoring the broken and missing pieces of our wholeness and creating a community of shalom in which each image bearer finds their truest self in their relational connection with God and fellow image bearers.

A church that lives in the neighborhood like this would be an authentic parable of God's intentions—a demonstration plot of the kingdom—inviting the world to experience God's shalom for themselves.

So, how do we cultivate the *other* of God's tomorrow in the midst of our every day?

To begin, we need strategies and practices that start and work back from *God's tomorrow*. In other words, we need a serious flesh-and-blood eschatology. We have failed to develop an eschatological imagination robust enough to work its way into how we understand our current day. For too long, eschatology has been relegated to end-times speculation or sentimental notions we cling to when times are tough. Instead of this, our eschatological vision has got to be sharpened, understanding that the present-future reality of the kingdom of God invites us to discern and act out our entire way of life by its light.

This means, for example, that our preaching needs to not only connect people to the Jesus of the Gospels (which it certainly does) but also to integrate the eschatological realities of God revealed throughout Scripture. Consider the words God spoke to the people through the prophet Zechariah;

> The word of the Lord Almighty came to me.
> This is what the LORD Almighty says: "I am very jealous for Zion; I am burning with jealousy for her."

This is what the LORD says: "I will return to Zion and dwell in Jerusalem. Then Jerusalem will be called the Faithful City, and the mountain of the LORD Almighty will be called the Holy Mountain."

This is what the LORD Almighty says: "Once again men and women of ripe old age will sit in the streets of Jerusalem, each of them with cane in hand because of their age. The city streets will be filled with boys and girls playing there."

This is what the LORD Almighty says: "It may seem marvelous to the remnant of this people at that time, but will it seem marvelous to me?" declares the LORD Almighty. (Zechariah 8:1-6)

I'm struck here by the language of the future (eschatological) experience of shalom and the way these future promises work to create a new imaginative space out of which the people are able to make sense of their present way of life. The people will live a radically different way in their present because of the future promises. This is the work of creating theological imagination through the proclamation of God's future intentions. A serious commitment to this kind of work in the life of a congregation creates significant possibilities for the way of life in that community, especially if pastors and leaders are intentional about drawing straightforward lines of connection for folks.

Helping people land these ancient prophetic visions of God's tomorrow in the dirt of their everyday lives is a critical and invigorating task. Preaching through Zechariah 8, I took the opportunity to do a kind of midrash work in the middle of the sermon, rewriting and reimagining the text in our context with imagery and language common to us in our place. It was supposed to be a fun example and a bit of novelty that kept me engaged in my sermon prep, so I was surprised at the response it got within our church. Probably more than any other single example, this provoked people to conversation, imagination, and the kind of eschatological vision we would need to think about what God might want to do in our community. I'm not sure I'd do this every week, but the way people drank from Zechariah's vision when they had a new kind of access to it left an impression on me.

Beyond the work of theology and preaching, what would change about the way we planned our ministries if we started with deep and robust reflection about what our neighborhoods would look like if they reflected the realities described in Revelation 21–22, for instance? We need to develop new Jerusalem eyes. It is easy to focus on the negative aspects of our communities, but what if, instead, we trained ourselves and our communities to walk around our communities asking God to reveal to us what it would look like if God's tomorrow showed up in concrete ways.

A few years ago I was leading a seminar on this topic at a local church in Michigan. We were exploring the Lord's Prayer together. In this prayer, Jesus teaches the disciples to pray "your kingdom come, . . . on earth as it is in heaven." If we understand this as Jesus teaching the disciples to long for God's kingdom (tomorrow) to show up on earth (today), then we can say that Jesus is giving us a specific practice through which we might stir our imaginations regarding what it means to be a people who embody God's intentions in the world.

After we explored this prayer together, we transitioned to the street. Armed with the language of the Lord's Prayer, we went out into the neighborhood and asked God to give us vision for what it would mean for this place and this time if the kingdom of God took root. After a couple of hours of walking around and asking God to give us a deeper imagination for his intentions, we gathered together to debrief the experience.

One of the men in the group spoke first. I remember holding my breath because I was skeptical at his level of engagement and quite frankly had prejudged him to be someone who would be skeptical of such an exercise. He had decided to get in his car and drive to the neighborhood where he had worked (in a local business) for nearly three decades. As he walked around the neighborhood praying, he had an experience he had never had before. To hear him tell it, he had spent nearly thirty years disliking his neighborhood because of its blight, its poverty, its "undesirable" people. However, as he walked around praying the Lord's Prayer he saw with new eyes. It was interesting that he didn't see *new* things, but the same things in a new way. Instead of only seeing blight and brokenness, he saw the distinct beauty and possibility.[13] He came back energized at the potential he witnessed (in just a ninety-minute exercise) of how God might want to bring shalom to that economically depressed neighborhood.

This is evidence of a deepening eschatological imagination. This man was growing in his ability to see himself and the church as a parable of God's intentions because he could for the first time in a generation picture God's tomorrow breaking into the present day. This is an example of how we begin to integrate the life and work of Jesus with the future reality of God's new creation where Jesus is "making everything new." This man saw his neighborhood that way for the very first time.

So, what would it look like to create rhythms of this in your congregational life? How might you create time and space to dream God's dream for your neighborhood together? No other single practice has invigorated congregations I've been a part of toward the radical shalom of God's tomorrow more than walking into the streets and prayerfully, expectantly *wondering* together what God's tomorrow would look like if it showed up today.

This kind of eschatological visioning *moves* us out into the neighborhood. It creates a sense of community that can help overcome the artificial divide between congregation and community. And it gives us the raw material to begin to think about how our way of life might spill out into the neighborhood in ways that work to express and extend God's shalom in the world.

QUESTIONS FOR CONSIDERATION

1. Are eschatological themes present in the way your church thinks about its identity and role in the world? What steps could you take to deepen the eschatological imagination of your congregation?

2. Where does your community need a demonstration of God's tomorrow? Are there ways your congregation might be positioned to creatively enact that reality?

3. There might be prework needed within your congregation. Creating a regular rhythm of being out in the community with expectant and prayerful eyes can help create an imagination for church as parable. How could you experiment with a kind of "on earth as it is in heaven" practice? What kind of ideas or insights arise as you do this together?

4. Praying the Lord's Prayer in our neighborhood can give us eyes to see possibility where we used to only see problems. What possibilities are you seeing that you've never noticed before?

4

GARDENERS OF SHALOM

THE CHURCH FOR FLOURISHING
AND TRANSFORMATION

What does it mean to be *for* something? I am a die-hard, well-past-borderline obsessed fan of the University of Notre Dame, the football team in particular. I live and die, and my wife will tell you that my mood rises and falls, with the fortunes of the Fighting Irish on the field. Over time, my closet accumulated a trove of branded gear, and I would wager I could count on one hand the number of days *in a year* that I don't wear some article of clothing that demonstrates my allegiance. I know the fight song by heart, taught it to my kids before (gulp) teaching them some of the most significant hymns, and cry every year when I watch *Rudy*. I could go on.

But that isn't what provides the most crystal-clear evidence that I root *for* Notre Dame. It's actually just a simple pronoun—*we*. Whenever I talk about the Irish, I use the *first person plural* to describe the team. I cannot help lumping myself in with the school. I didn't attend there, didn't play for the team, and am, much to my chagrin, not asked for feedback related to player development and program trajectory. But overwhelmingly I will say things like, "We have a good team this year. We really played well last week. We have a chance to make the playoffs this year." More than any amount of ND swag, or ability to quote the Alma Mater or whether or not I considered naming my daughter after Knute Rockne, this is, in my estimation, all the evidence I need to know that my identity is wrapped up in the identity of these sports teams. As I mentioned earlier, their fortunes on the field have become my fortunes in every way but reality.

I think this realization has helped me understand something fundamental about life. Being *for* something—or someone—is demonstrated by the extent to which the distance of *us and them* is erased to form *we*. As long as the language we use reflects a kind of relational distance, our level of investment will have room to grow. As long as we are *us and them*, we will not see our fortunes as tied up with the fortunes of the other person. When I say to my kids, "I am for you," what I am indicating is that there is no relational distance between us. The two of us are *we*. Their struggles are my struggles; we experience them together, albeit in different ways. Their joys and celebrations become my joys and celebrations—just watch me watch them on a baseball diamond. Our fortunes are bound up together in a way that is wholly unique and deeply powerful.

In all of life, it's actually pretty rare to experience the kind of intertwined relational dynamic that causes us to see ourselves as wrapped up—not codependent—in the lives of others. To be *for* someone such that we consider our fortunes bound up together, caught in a single garment of destiny, perhaps, is not something we experience with a great degree of frequency. But I think it is critical for us as the church to consider this notion deeply, particularly as we discern new ways of seeing related to the pursuit of justice and shalom in the world.

When I was pastoring, a small group of us were seeking to answer that question—what does it mean to be *for* a place—and to do so by demonstrating God's serious concern for folks who live at the margins of society and who are often overlooked by our community. To that end, we attempted to create job-development pathways for folks experiencing homelessness and other forms of crisis. The result was a fledgling social enterprise pie shop. Through the deliciously ordinary making of pies, we discovered a channel to challenge the way we devalue people who share our neighborhoods with us.

As we initially connected with our neighbors, we heard people articulating a sense of longing for a gathering space in the neighborhood. Many of the old spots had gone away, and there was a deep need for a place for people to be in relationship with each other. Helping to create a space like that would be one way we could demonstrate that we wanted our neighborhood to thrive as a reflection of God's desire to see the neighborhood thrive.

We made a ton of mistakes along the way and couldn't end up sustaining the business. But the two years we were working on this project, connecting with neighbors, facilitating job training and networking for people in crisis, clarified a serious conviction for me. A church that authentically and faithfully extends God's shalom into the world will most likely do so because it has decided it is *for* its place the same way I am *for* the Fighting Irish. We cannot faithfully seek justice unless we seriously grapple with the notion of what it means to be *for* something, namely, the place God has put us and the people we share that space with.

This notion of church *for* something (in this case the flourishing and transformation of people and place) provides a telos point toward which we can move as we seek to live out of and into our identity as the church.

Inhabit the rabbit. In one of the most famous scenes of *Monty Python and the Holy Grail*, our beleaguered protagonists have "galloped" their way up to the base of a large castled city in search of their sacred relic. In a memorable exchange of increasingly silly insults, the knights realize that they are at odds with the inhabitants of the fortress city. After a series of failed frontal assaults (*run away!*) they take cover behind a large berm some distance away from the city to plot their next move. They decide (à la the Trojan Horse) to construct a giant wooden rabbit, which they will wheel up to the gate of the city in the hopes that those inside will welcome it and bring the rabbit inside the city walls. They watch from a distance as their plan works to perfection, the rabbit is presented and accepted, and then they wait. One of the knights asks what happens next and another responds "Lancelot, Galahad, and I will leap out of the rabbit and take the city by force!" As he continues to repeat the plan, they realize that they have forgotten the key element: they never got inside the rabbit. Their failure is all too clear as they watch their hard work go to waste *from a distance.*

The church is often more akin to the knights of Monty Python than we'd like to admit, trying—in fits and starts—to assail society with frontal assaults. We are often ridiculed for it, so we retreat to a safe distance. A significant part of our history in evangelicalism could be characterized by either full-frontal assault on society or distancing ourselves in a protectionist way. Over time, thankfully, many of us have come to see that neither approach is particularly Jesus shaped, and neither is effective in any way in the pursuit of God's mission in the world. And so we have attempted to re-engage society. Much of the megachurch, church planting, missional, and emergent conversations over the last twenty to thirty years have been an attempt to navigate the tension between all-out assault and huddling up at safe distances.

The same could be said for the work of justice. Churches long engaged in the work of justice would likely not resonate with these tensions, but for many of us in the predominately white evangelical world, engaging the most broken places in our world has tended to look like assault or retreat. Our evangelical corrective to this within the justice world has still produced Monty Python-esque results. It is not uncommon for churches to have incredibly compassionate hearts for people who experience life at the margins of their city. We want to demonstrate the love of Christ, so we drive across town once a week and run a program of some sort. We want to provide help and assistance, and in increasing numbers we want to engage the issues that are causing the problems in the first place. This all has the potential to be a faithful expression and extension of God's shalom in the world. The problem is that an overwhelming number of us still do that work from a distance. This distance, leaders engaged in this work will tell you, exponentially increases the challenges of building relationships of mutuality, developing equitable leadership structures, fostering trust, and so on. The challenges we face when we work from a distance are the same challenges we face trying to do anything from a distance. It requires a level of consistency and vigilance few people or groups can sustain, and even then the work is more prone to growing apart than together. The creative gift we offer up to our community is one we fail to embody, and so we watch our efforts struggle *from a distance.* This is the distance between *us and them* and *we.* In short, we fail to inhabit the rabbit.

Inhabit the rabbit: church for its place. The *distance* we allow between us and the community we are engaging is the extent to which we will fail to truly be for the place God has put us. That distance (relational, geographic, cultural, socioeconomic) creates barriers that will undercut our attempts to engage meaningfully. It will result in programmatic approaches to justice that exhaust people and resources along the way. This is not to say that nothing good or redemptive can come from our best efforts—even if they come from a distance. But allowing ourselves to remain distant from the community will undermine even the best intentions and will make it challenging to see good fruit come in the long run.

We need to get to a place where *us and them* become *we*. We can cultivate the kind of relational dynamic with the place and the people where the distance between parties is overcome and replaced with a kind of mutuality of identity. Nowhere is this outlined more clearly than in Jeremiah 29.

> This is what the LORD Almighty, the God of Israel, says to all those I carried into exile from Jerusalem to Babylon: "Build houses and settle down; plant gardens and eat what they produce. Marry and have sons and daughters; find wives for your sons and give your daughters in marriage, so that they too may have sons and daughters. Increase in number there; do not decrease. Also, seek the peace and prosperity of the city to which I have carried you into exile. Pray to the LORD for it, because if it prospers, you too will prosper." (Jeremiah 29:4-7)

In this passage, God has a very specific vision in mind. The call of God to seek the peace (shalom) of Babylon has practical implications (see chap. 6), but it also contains implications for the people's posture and perspective. For one, God indicates that the fortunes of Israel are bound up with the fortunes of Babylon. In verse 7, Jeremiah directly connects this notion of being *for* a place with the intertwining of the people's fortunes. To say "pray to the Lord *for* it, because if it prospers, you too will prosper" is to advocate the idea we've been exploring all along.

This idea of praying for the city is interesting because, if I'm being honest, sometimes I use the language "I'll pray for you" to maintain relational distance! Not maliciously or with forethought, but I have come to notice, regretfully, that I tell people I will pray for them far more often than I actually pray for them. There have been times when I tell people I will pray for them, feel the Spirit's nudge to do so with them right there, but still move on to the rest of my day. Perhaps I'm not alone in noticing that in my more self-centered moments I find myself *further* away from a person or situation because my promise to pray acted more like a stiff-arm than an embrace of the other. God intends just the opposite. To pray for a city, in this case Babylon, is not to offer empty promises that create distance; instead, it serves to increase Israel's capacity to embrace Babylon. Think about that! God is calling Israel to a posture toward the city that will drastically cut down the relational distance and will effectively serve to help Israel embrace this thoroughly pagan place.

God says *pray for* Babylon because your prosperity is tied up together. Developing the idea that seeking the shalom of the city cannot be done from a position of relational distance, God is saying that because what they get, you will get—and what you get, they will get—you should figure out how to want the same things. As Dennis Edwards says, "Jeremiah said what amounts to a slogan: 'As Babylon's life goes, so goes your life!'"[1]

Chicago pastor Jonathan Brooks says that the idea here is that what I want for my kids, I should want for all the kids in the community.[2] I resonate with this because as a parent I have a lot of desires for my kids. When my sons were six and four, they began playing summer league baseball. As a kid, I had some bad experiences with coaches, and as the season drew near I felt my level of anxiety increasing as I pictured them learning to play baseball under the guidance of some crazy, maniacal "win at all costs" kind of coach. So, while I had no real positive desire to do so, I signed up to coach their teams as a way of making sure that their coach (me) wouldn't ruin baseball for them, and I wouldn't spend the summer losing my mind watching it happen!

Surprisingly, God used these summer league evenings to teach me the lesson we read about in Jeremiah. The league our kids were in was full of kids who experienced life in a much different way from my kids. Many had unstable family situations, dealt with food insecurity, and had insufficient educational opportunity, and over time I observed that these kids on my team had experienced very little in terms of real shalom in their lives. I came to see that if I were to continue coaching, just for the sake of my kids' experience, I would miss an opportunity to see this the right way. Instead of wanting my kids to flourish, God was teaching me—however thickheaded I was along the way—that the better perspective was to want *all* these kids to experience shalom. If my entire team experienced shalom through our experience together, then my boys would not be left out of that. If I focused all that effort on my two sons, then all the other kids would suffer as a result. To focus on my two sons alone would function to stiff-arm the rest of these kids and their families, but I was learning how to embrace these families and see our lives as intertwined.

In short, God is calling Israel to see *us and them* as *we* and to recognize that, in fact, *we are all in this together*. Given that, God's call is to seek the peace and prosperity of the city. Peace or shalom—the idea that *nothing is missing and nothing is broken*—suggests that Israel's call is to pursue God's intentions for the city. The very fact that shalom needs to be *sought* means that within Babylon some things are missing and broken. The work of seeking shalom should be seen as a work of restoration and redemption. Because the most comprehensive translation of the word *shalom* is "wholeness," we could read this text as God inviting Israel to work to make Babylon whole. I wonder what might be different in our national political narrative if we were concerned with making America whole instead of pursuing some artificially constructed notion of greatness.

Prosperity is a tricky word for us because we are likely to read it through the modern American and capitalist lens. In that vein, prosperity is about the accumulation of wealth. There are many who struggle with this text because of this kind of reading or many who would advocate for the virtue of unconsidered wealth accumulation in light of it. I think there is a much more ordinary—human—way of thinking about this word *prosperity* that has more to do with the notion of flourishing.

Thinking of this in agricultural terms, if a gardener says that a seed has *prospered*, they are not talking about wealth accumulation but the idea of potential and abundance. A garden prospers when the seed takes root, blooms, grows strong, and produces fruit. A garden prospers when that potential yield is abundant or more than expected, not because it represents profit but because the seeds themselves did something surprising and worthy of celebration.

This is why the ancient harvest festivals (first fruits, for example) were so significant. Israel wasn't celebrating a yield that would turn a profit, they were celebrating the realized potential, *in abundance*, of the seed they had planted some months ago. The word we should land on when thinking about prosperity is *flourishing*. It's a word we've been using all along, and that is because I think it gets to this idea in a critical way. When we say a person is flourishing in something, we mean they have realized some potential that has been

cultivated along the way. What's more, when a person is truly flourishing, people take note and get excited because the fruit coming
from their labor and life is *more than* what was expected. Human
flourishing lives at this intersection of potential and abundance.

It's no wonder to me that Jeremiah 29 is the banner text for urban
ministry and justice workers. There is a level of richness to this vision
of Israel being a people *in exile* who, rather than create relational
distance, are called to see their lives as authentically intertwined with
the society around them and to then proactively and intentionally
work to see that the broken pieces of the city and its people are put
back together in such a way that the city and its people experience
human flourishing; Babylon and Israel together—*we*.

Why does this matter? If we hope to be the church that God intends, which expresses and extends God's shalom into the world,
then it is critical that we consider the implications of being a church
for flourishing and transformation particularly alongside the poor,
marginalized, and vulnerable neighbors in our community.[3] Flourishing cannot truly exist in a world that incarcerates an irrespon-
sible and compassionless percentage of the black population. There
cannot be wholeness in a community wracked by violence; nor can
there be wholeness in a neighborhood where human dignity is
denied by unjust policing. People do not flourish when they cannot
afford stable housing and when lending practices exclude the most
vulnerable from the stabilizing effects of homeownership. Pursuing
shalom for the people, and in the places of brokenness God has put
us in and among, is the beginning work of justice.

Without a commitment to seeking the shalom and flourishing
of the city and its people, justice work becomes disembodied and
idealistic. Seeking to give tangible expression to God's shalom
is a barometer of our faithfulness to God and a primary way we

demonstrate God's tomorrow to the world. Consider the words of Jesus in Matthew 25. Having separated the sheep (faithful ones) from the goats (unfaithful ones) he describes how their faithfulness was evidenced.

> Come, you who are blessed by my Father; take your inheritance, the kingdom prepared for you since the creation of the world. For I was hungry and you gave me something to eat, I was thirsty and you gave me something to drink, I was a stranger and you invited me in, I needed clothes and you clothed me, I was sick and you looked after me, I was in prison and you came to visit me. (Matthew 25:34-36)

We quote Matthew 25 to the point of cliché on this topic, but it is hard to ignore the straightforward way Jesus draws a line between faithfulness and the intentional pursuit of shalom. Many years later, Jesus' brother James comes to a similar conclusion: "Religion that God our Father accepts as pure and faultless is this: to look after orphans and widows in their distress and to keep oneself from being polluted by the world" (James 1:27). Seeking shalom and flourishing in the broken places of our communities is not the only measure of our faithfulness, but it is essential and first among the priorities of the Jesus community we read about in the New Testament.

Isaiah 58 is another hallmark text regarding God's heart for justice. I've preached it many times. Every time I do, I probably take too much delight channeling God's frustration at the people's complacency and complicity in relational and systemic injustice. One time, preaching this text with all the fervor I could muster, I got an unexpected response from someone in my church. Later that day, he texted me—quoting Isaiah 58:12:

Your people will rebuild the ancient ruins
     and will raise up the age-old foundations;
you will be called Repairer of Broken Walls,
     Restorer of Streets with Dwellings.

The text said, "I want to be a Repairer of Broken Walls." I'll never forget it. I'm captivated by the imagery here. After all the commands to root out injustice and to deeply and thoroughly orient their way of life around the pursuit of God's shalom and justice, we get this verse that seems to suggest that the pursuit of justice in and through the community *will result in meaningful flourishing and transformation.* In other words, when God's people seek shalom, God's people should expect to see shalom. When we seek the flourishing of the city, it's not a fool's errand or idealistic do-goodery. Instead, a straightforward reading seems to indicate that God calls the people to pursue these ends because God is going to use the people to achieve these ends.

I'm struck by the transformational outcomes that come to characterize the people of God. This notion of being known as a people who repair and restore (to the point that nothing is missing and nothing is broken) is not a legacy in the sense of self-adulation. It seems to me that this is simply an admission on the part of God that if the people will just be just, they will be involved in the cultivation of shalom such that people and communities will flourish as a result. Here in this text Isaiah envisions the people's justice seeking as having a comprehensive, transformative effect. A by-product of a faithful way of life is a realized transformation of the place, one which encompasses every corner of a society (people, culture, systems, built environment, creation itself). This is how the church demonstrates the kingdom intentions of God. We don't establish the kingdom ourselves, but if we are for a place to the extent that we see this kind of transformation, we've demonstrated it for people to see, touch, taste, and smell. This helps us resist the problematic notion that the kingdom of God is experienced in merely abstracted, spiritual ways. God's intentions include the total renewal of all things; our demonstration of that future should seek to be equally tangible and concrete.

I have a hard time reading passages like the ones we have considered so far and thinking that the purpose of the church is not intimately connected with the proactive, passionate, and intentional pursuit of shalom where God has placed us. It is impossible for me to read these kinds of passages and think that God is ambivalent about our concern for the lived experience of the most vulnerable folks in our midst. The idea of being a church for flourishing and transformation is a map to give us direction as we attempt to navigate the world as God's people toward the ends of God.

So, what are we for? If we were to take this seriously, it will force us to deal with what we are for now. Isaiah 58 helps us wrestle with this question. At the start of the chapter the outcome being produced was injustice, relational and structural. That revealed something about Israel's life together; namely, they had grossly misunderstood what faithfulness meant. Conversely, at the end of the text, we see the outcome of transformation, restoration, renewal—shalom. Those outcomes demonstrate that instead of being for mere religious practice, the people would shift to being for justice and shalom.

This is the work we will need to do in our churches. If we want to know what we are *for*, we need only look at the outcomes we are producing. Even more revealing than the outcomes alone, we gain much insight into what we are *for* when we examine *why* we measure the outcomes we do, to begin with.

It is here that the evangelical church has a great opportunity for growth. If you are a pastor or have spent any time in a group of pastors, you will observe quickly the outcomes we are shooting for and the metrics we use to measure those outcomes. It seems that anytime I find myself in the company of fellow clergy, we all start falling into patterns of talking about the stereotypical numbers, budgets, and buildings.

In *The Lean Startup*, Eric Ries argues that businesses often find ways of running their numbers that give the impression of business success, but actually say very little about the outcomes of the business. He calls these measures vanity metrics.[4] For me, this idea clarifies the problems with the way we measure success in the church.

Consider how we give evidence of the success of programs in the church. Isn't participation the most commonly used evaluation metric? This happens in traditional church programs but also most of the programs we employ for the sake of the work of justice. We had this many people attend, we had this many volunteers, we had this many visitors, we had this many kids in our after-school program, we gave away this many pounds of food, representing this many families in the community. The participation numbers go on and on. Do I think it's wrong to count? Not at all. But counting essentially proves nothing if we cannot at the same time talk about what has happened because of that participation.

Saying that we have two hundred, five hundred, or one thousand people at church on Sunday doesn't, on its own, give evidence of anything of kingdom substance. In the same way, being able to say that we gave away, say, three hundred backpacks is a vanity metric because it blurs the line of resource flow and actual transformation. We haven't demonstrated that anyone or anything is experiencing the shalom of God by the simple tallying of participation or attendance.

Set next to the goal of the flourishing and transformation of people and place, how can I be content to merely count heads coming through my door?

Of course, it's not always like this, but vanity metrics tempt us to use numbers to give the impression of success, and a preoccupation with numbers (people, money, participation, etc.) will make success subservient to our own ends. In other words, vanity metrics almost always become an exercise in navel gazing. They are most often used to validate the amount of energy we've expended. If it takes me twenty-five hours to plan and execute a worship service, I will certainly feel better about that time expenditure if one thousand people experience it rather than fifty. Similarly, if I've gone through the effort of organizing a food or coat drive and only five people stand in line, I'm prone to think the only way it could have been better is if more people came through. I often observe how easy it is for us in ministry to use these vanity metrics as a way of shoring up our sense of identity or security as ministers, rather than using evaluation metrics that force me to look beyond the end of my own nose—or beyond the walls of my own church—and consider the impact our efforts have in the actual place and in the lives of the actual people God has placed us alongside.

Contrast that sense of inevitable self-centeredness brought on by vanity metrics with the outward looking, transformative vision of Isaiah. Imagine what might change for a church who steadfastly refused to be swayed by vanity metrics and *instead* decided that success would be the outcome of flourishing and transformation? We aren't "successful" unless we can be called repairers of broken walls. If we want to be a church for justice and the flourishing of our neighbors and neighborhood, then we need new ways of determining whether we are on the right track.

Gardeners of shalom: Cultivating flourishing and transformation.
When gardeners enter the greenhouse to work, they are one of a
myriad of factors that affect the plants inside. Gardeners play a specific role in the greenhouse, and a major part of that work is understanding the spaces in which they can and cannot affect change. The
work of gardening in a greenhouse is not about *dominance and control.*
Instead, the work is to *cultivate* an ecosystem that promotes the
flourishing of each individual plant. Any direct engagement on the
part of the gardener is targeted and is for the benefit of the most
vulnerable plants in the greenhouse. Recognizing that all of the potential for fruitfulness in each individual plant was present in the
seed of that plant, the point of gardening is not to *create* the fruit in
each seed but to *nurture* the abundance that lies in each seed by
targeted care. It is a work of tending to the overall environment,
creating the conditions for each seed to flourish, and then paying
attention to the specific factors causing particular seeds to struggle
and mitigating those as much as possible.

*Pastoring the parish: Blurring lines between congregation and
community.* The picture of gardeners cultivating an ecosystem so
that every seed can flourish helps me frame the place of church in
a neighborhood. It is a work of mutual cultivation in community.
For pastors, an important part of the role is blurring the lines between congregation and community. Historically, we have tended
to draw a hard-and-fast distinction between what happens in the
narthex and what happens in the neighborhood. Not only will this
reinforce the unhelpful idea that seeking God's shalom justice is a
work that happens "out there," it also creates a divided way of
thinking about the role of shepherd in a community. The more
rooted we are in a place, the more we embrace the notion of *we*—
demonstrating that we are for the *place* God has put us and for the

people we share those spaces with—the more natural it will become to see our work as pastoring the parish of our neighborhood. When I walk around a neighborhood with a pastor who not only knows facts about the community but who knows the names, families, and stories of the people who share the neighborhood with them, I know I'm in the presence of a parish pastor.

Pastoring a parish means that whether we are in our church or out in the community, we work as gardeners in a greenhouse. We tend the overall parish environment, working to cultivate the conditions for flourishing and paying attention to the specific factors causing particular individuals, families, or groups to struggle. As we observe the specific kinds of vulnerabilities people experience in our neighborhood, our work can become more targeted to address the underlying causes of vulnerability until the ecosystem is brought back into balance. Our work is not to dominate or control (e.g., come in with all the answers) but to cultivate a neighborhood ecosystem that promotes the flourishing (to abundance!) of each individual and family.

This is why economic and community development makes so much sense for the local community of faith committed to being a conduit of shalom. Because it is the work of cultivating a healthy neighborhood ecosystem—where individuals, families, and even the place itself can flourish as God intends—it helps us shoulder the burden of a broken world in need of restoration and renewal. We are a people who tend to what God's given us to tend, trusting that God will bring about the fruit of wholeness, flourishing, and transformation as we faithfully cultivate toward those ends.

This is the hope for any church engaging in true economic and community development. Churches are able to engage the particularity of their place and the people who live there for the purpose of seeing the fruit of real flourishing. This work doesn't have to devolve into familiar patterns of paternalism or be complicated by unhealthy power dynamics, because we do this work knowing that ultimately we too are in need of our neighbors. Our fortunes are bound up together (Jeremiah 29), and we know that we cannot flourish unless our neighbors flourish. Ultimately, the work of healthy economic and community development is one of mutuality and reciprocity. It puts our money where our mouth is as we pursue the kinship of the shalom community in the neighborhood God has placed us.

WHERE DO WE START?

My friend Chris—who pastors a church in Indiana—is the definition of a parish pastor. The church is located in a school in the part of town most likely to be sidestepped by folks without a kingdom vision. But this is a church with a kingdom vision and a parish perspective. So, when they do their work of envisioning what God might want for their community, the community is part of that work. Specifically, over a series of monthly potlucks, church members and neighbors gathered together to talk about the issues confronting the neighborhood and to imagine a different future together. The neighbors didn't always have the right theological language to describe their dreams, and the language of the gospel wasn't always on their lips, but that is what the congregation is for. The church becomes interpreters of God's *mañana* in a community where the language of the kingdom is at best a second language.

As these meetings unfolded, with gentle and humble guidance from the leaders of this church, some common objectives emerged. They found ways of collaborating for the flourishing and transformation of the place they shared. The church never surrendered its status as a prophetically alternative community, and it took seriously the call to demonstrate God's intentions, and along the way they discovered how to authentically be *we* with their friends and neighbors outside the church. They are all in it together, seeking the peace of their city, praying to God for their city because they know if it prospers, they too will prosper.

Seeking the flourishing and transformation of the place God has put you, particularly in places of great vulnerability or with people who have been pushed to the margins, can give the ignited imagination of your congregation a pathway to put inspiration into action. The way this work gets done is critical, so it is important to think well through issues of *how* you do this work, not just *what* work you are doing. Remembering the essential mutuality of this work as outlined in Jeremiah 29 is one way we can guard against the unhealthy paternalism that can accompany the ministry of a church in a neighborhood. With that in mind, consider these questions as you begin to discern a vision for the flourishing and transformation of your community and the neighbors you share this place with.

QUESTIONS FOR CONSIDERATION

1. What is your congregation for? How do you know?

2. Do you notice ways where you subtly create distance between your church and neighborhood? What dynamics are making that happen? How might you start to mitigate those?

3. What do you measure in your church? What does that reveal about the priorities of your congregation? How does that help or hinder the cultivation of God's shalom justice?

4. Is there a way you feel like your congregation falls into the temptation to use vanity metrics to create a sense of success? What changes can you make to resist that?

5. If you used the notion of flourishing and transformation of people and place as a benchmark, what would your measures of success look like?

6. For pastors, when you think about your normal patterns week to week, how could you adjust your schedule to begin blurring the line between congregation and community? What would pastoring the parish of your neighborhood look like in your context?

7. It's pretty rare to witness churches who authentically celebrate the potential and abundance of their neighborhoods. What would it look like for your church to make regular practices of joining in, or hosting, community celebrations of the beauty and possibility of your community?

PART 2

JUSTICE IN OUR CONGREGATIONAL LIFE

5

LOW-GROUND CHURCH

DISCERNING VISION IN A HIGH-GROUND WORLD

In part two, we are making a shift from theological frames to examining how those frames get worked out on the ground in various ways in the life of a local congregation. This isn't a treatise on the concrete work of justice in the world (there are scores of wonderful resources that can help you with this) as much as it is an examination of our normative patterns in congregational life. If we are going to cultivate a way of life where God's shalom can take root and bear fruit, then it is critical to think about the work of being the church and how we might tend to the ecosystem of our congregation so that the capacity for justice is enhanced and not diminished.

This begins with the way we cast vision and do strategic planning. In my work, I regularly notice the way seeking God's shalom functions as an appendage to the central mission of the local church rather than as an integrated thread of any common life in the church. This is where we find ourselves delegating, compartmentalizing, and deprioritizing the work of justice. This makes the communal pursuit of God's shalom incredibly difficult to lean into faithfully. If we want to see our church become a more just church, it is imperative that we think through how to integrate justice into our field of view when it comes to discerning the vision for our church.

I once pastored a congregation that looked a lot like any other church in the community. Among the usual assortment of ministry programs, we desired to demonstrate the love of Jesus to others in tangible ways. During a serious season of vision discernment, many on our leadership team wanted to center our church's outreach vision around the language Jesus reads from Isaiah in Luke 4. But we got a bit off-track after a while because we fell into the pattern of lumping any "external" work in the community under the banner of the vision Jesus proclaims in this text. So we paused and tried to wrestle with the real implications of such a formative text. What does it mean that Jesus centers what is essentially his inaugural address—declaring the intentions for his kingdom—on the poor and the oppressed? In a relatively affluent congregation, what might it mean that Jesus seems to have an overriding concern for the poor?

We began to question whether everything could be labeled "Luke 4" work. As the conversation continued—a bit heated at this point— we were at odds over whether that was a fundamentally exclusive way of speaking. The essential question seemed to be, when an up-wardly mobile person hears that our focus is on the poor and mar-ginalized, won't they feel left out? Admittedly, even though I was, and still am, pretty committed to the notion that a preference for the poor is essential, I was probably not doing a great job of demon-strating any concern for the wealthier members of our congregation. At one point in the conversation, I tried to emphasize my view that in Luke 4, Jesus is acknowledging his bias toward the poor and marginalized when he says, "The Spirit of the Lord is on me / be-cause he has anointed me / to proclaim good news to the poor," at which point one of our leaders turned to me and said *"and the rich!"*

I learned two things at that moment. First, I can be pretty bull-headed and obtuse when it comes to conversations like this. I really don't think my colaborer was mad at Jesus or was necessarily arguing against the point, but was increasingly frustrated with me and the (probably) fundamentalist tone I was taking in the course of the conversation.

Second, I learned that anytime we want to make some definitive point in this conversation on justice, we are going to upset the status quo. That moment is a pastoral work when it happens in the context of the local congregation. It's not an argument to win, it's a reality to be explored and embraced together as we journey deeper into God's kingdom in community. I had allowed it to be a contest of wills rather than the space to discern God's heart for justice that we talked about in chapter three.

Our ongoing wrestling with this Luke 4 language revealed that if we were going to be a church in authentic pursuit of justice, we would have to find a way to talk about God's overriding concern for the poor and oppressed that didn't exclude people needlessly. I felt that if I could resist devolving into antagonisms myself, there might be a way forward. I understand the supposed point that Jesus actually does care about everyone. Of course he does. But, similar to the work being done when people use the phrase "No, All Lives Matter!" we were in a moment when we were tempted to miss the nuance that would open the door to God's shalom. Lumping everyone together missed the point Jesus was making and would serve to sweep the real implications of our faith under the rug in favor of an expression of faith that allowed people to remain unchallenged, in this case, regarding their wealth in a world of inequity. At the moment, I didn't have a theological imagination big enough to shepherd us through the conversation.

Giving shape to a vision that centers on the pursuit of God's shalom is difficult work. It will undoubtedly upset the status quo of the congregation. The instability that it will create should be tended to thoughtfully in order to resist both giving into collective fragility and needlessly steamrolling people in the process. Admittedly, this chapter is pretty frank related to the vision of our churches and its impact on our pursuit of justice. My hope is that this conversation helps us lean into the necessary correctives for our local lives in community.

SEEK FIRST THE HIGH GROUND?

The first house my wife and I bought was situated at the foot of a relatively large hill at the edge of the St. Joseph River Valley in northern Indiana. Our neighborhood sat on land that had been filled in for development but which had been a floodplain for the river. In short, our house was built on a bog. And there was a good reason for calling it a floodplain. Every time it rained, the water would rush down the slope of the hill to our south and run toward the river, thereby forming a new river that went right through our backyard. I had wondered as we looked at the home with our realtor why the basement had *two* sump pumps; now I knew. The falling rain threatened our house; even light rains had a significant impact on our property. I returned home after every vacation expecting to find a flooded basement. In fact, just a few weeks after we moved out of that house an enormous rainstorm occurred that severely affected scores of families living in the bog valley. Not surprisingly, the houses on the hill were untouched. They were relatively impervious to this kind of disaster.

It's a common theme of history (and I suppose Sunday school songs) that houses on high ground are to be preferred to houses on the low ground, which are significantly more vulnerable to the storms of life. Because occupying the low ground puts people in a vulnerable space, it makes sense that people congregate on the high ground. The high ground is not only safer and more resilient to external threats, but it is also strategically advantageous because in a situation where you find yourself in conflict with another person, having the high ground gives you the upper hand.

The high-ground dynamic is mirrored across society as well. The people who live in the "lowest" places in our society are most vulnerable to the rising waters of life's storms. These are the folks Jesus referred to as the "least," the ones without the natural advantages of those who occupy the societal high ground.

Just as people have aspired to occupy the physical high ground, people aim to occupy the social high ground as well. And for the same reasons.

It is safer to live on the social high ground. When we moved to Chicago, our realtor made a lot of suggestions for us as we looked for an apartment and tried to figure out a good neighborhood to move to. The vast majority of those suggestions were related to safety. The assumption that no one would choose to live in a violent place was self-evident. This is the high-ground versus low-ground dynamic at work. In a high-ground society, safety is a priority. Thus, folks with the means to live in a high-ground world have the capacity to protect their borders and defend themselves against all threats.[1]

At the same time, occupying the social high ground is strategically advantageous because the high ground is where the movers and the shakers live, work, and play. We live in a world where it's strategically advantageous to be close to those kind of folks in those kind of places, making the social high ground an attractive place to be—and for folks who don't find themselves there, it's an attractive place to *aspire* to be.

The cultural forces of our day reinforce the implicit and assumed virtue of pursuing the high ground and maintaining our footing there at all costs. This is the inner logic of capitalism and consumerism: upward mobility is of unquestionable virtue, or at the very least upward mobility is amoral and so can be prioritized without regard to its implications for, or effect on, the world. As a result, we live in a world that almost wholly centers on the experience, values, physical space, and felt needs of the movers and the shakers, the folks who occupy the social high ground.

So, a question. What would it look like if the church centered its world on the experience, values, physical space, and felt needs of society's movers and shakers? What would a high-ground church look like?

In other words, *what would a prosperity gospel for the already prosperous look like?* In my mind, a prosperity gospel for the upwardly mobile would not need to proclaim the promises of wealth yet unattained; instead, it would proclaim *permission* for wealth already achieved. It would make the upwardly mobile feel unchallenged in their wealth and would seek to articulate a brand of Christianity that integrated seamlessly into an American society of upward mobility, consumerism, and success. The built environment of these churches would not need to be unduly flashy by the world's terms; instead, they would simply need to feel homey to the richest in our midst. In creating church environments that are familiar and comfortable for the wealthy, we affirm the pursuit and attainment of wealth and affluence. The American evangelical church has trafficked in a kind of prosperity gospel for at least a generation, and the evidence of this is seen in the way we do church today.

There is a battle for the soul of the church (and every local church), and it revolves around the pursuit of the high ground.

Human nature doesn't get checked at the door of our communities of faith. We bring our humanness into community with us. This means that every church is tempted to be a community that pursues the high ground in both physical place and social space.

I see this happening in our churches today in two primary ways.

Franchise church. While I can appreciate the potential logistical advantages to franchising a model of church as it relates to administration, overhead, and the creation of a leader-development pipeline, franchise models of church are one of the primary ways we orient church around the experience of the movers and shakers. The franchise model of church operates by the same principle of any franchise business, namely, that name recognition gives people a sense of familiarity and trust related to the product being sold inside. If I like the Chipotle restaurant in my town, I know I will like the Chipotle restaurant in your town. Similarly, if my local site of Gen X Church meets all my needs but I have to move somewhere, I can look for a site of Gen X Church in my new town. The expansion of the franchise, in some sense, depends on the mobility and transience of the church member, which naturally tends to favor movers and shakers.

Christianity for cool kids. A second way the American evangelical church seeks the high ground in our day is seen in what I call Christianity for cool kids. Hipster churches, in other words. There is a tidal wave of churches these days that places an exceedingly high priority on being relevant, cool, and hip churches for people who don't like church.

Using aesthetically hip and trendy cultural forms and injecting cool into the ethos of a community self-evidently appeals to a particular group of folks. These days, cool is a commodity packaged and repackaged with each passing year. It puts us into an unending cycle of keeping up with the Joneses.

These might seem like two different things (franchise church and Christianity for cool kids) but they share similar DNA in that both center on the experience—and cater to the values—of high-ground folks. Both expressions of church need to be in proximity to and relationship with the powerful, popular, and influential. This works to *exclude* folks who occupy the low ground.

In a franchise church, this is an issue of sustaining the model. It probably goes without saying but if your church strategy is to franchise a model of church into X number of communities over X number of years, you will need money to do that. Thus, the franchise-model church will have to work to attract high-ground folks because they have the resources needed to sustain the movement.

Even those churches that articulate a desire to do justice will, upon closer review, likely articulate a vision that tries to *empower people to do justice*, because the assumption is that the people being gathered are well positioned to create change in society. Unfortunately, the franchise-church model can unwittingly overlook people who don't have power, position, or influence, not necessarily because of ill intent but because it applies the same inner logic of prioritizing the high ground that society does. In a world like ours, it is assumed that folks who occupy the low ground are simply less capable than those who occupy the high ground, and the success of a franchise depends on developing "high capacity" leaders.

In cool-kid church, the same dynamic is at work. Because cool church is creating a culture that reflects and defines the cultural moment of "cool," there is a clear sense that church is oriented around the experience and sensibility of those who fit that mold. In his book *Race and Place*, David Leong considers this notion of hipster church and the way that it places at the center folks who occupy the cultural and aesthetic high ground. Contrary to the belief that the pursuit of hipster expressions of culture and church, can happen amorally, Leong concludes that "hipsterism is essentially trapped in a perpetual state of exclusion; that which is deemed uncool is to be rejected in favor of the shifting markers of whatever is trending. For many caught up in the aesthetics of cool, it's a hamster wheel of consumer accessorizing, but the costs of that consumption are paid for by their neighbors on the margins."[2] At issue here is not whether skinny jeans are okay to wear but the collateral damage of cool in communities that seek to grapple with the dynamics of the high and low ground. Christianity for cool kids is not only inherently exclusive, it prioritizes the values and aspirations of the high ground by creating a space where our consumptive quests go unchallenged. Hip church then creates further problems by marketing itself, often implicitly, in this manner. Again Leong is instructive here.

> Slicker marketing and so-called innovations in the church have largely failed to examine their assumptions about the appeal of cool. . . . Cool Christians are finding themselves caught in hipsterism's perpetual state of exclusion through adopting brand identities that implicitly create hierarchy and reject difference. The social and racial logic of cool, which contains various forms of cultural homogeneity, has been consumed instead of questioned.[3]

In the end, it doesn't matter if the conversation is about clothes, coffee, the Sunday morning vibe, or having a church with a progressive political disposition; the targeted audience in a cool church will always be centered on those who are hip enough to hang with the ethos of the congregation. There is simply no way to argue that you can try to be a cool, hip expression of church *and* resist centering folks on the high ground of society.

Making matters worse, if churches market a Christianity for cool kids using the progressive language of justice to demonstrate their relevance—pairing their justice language with a discernible ethos of cool—it gives the impression that justice is both an enlightened cosmopolitan worldview and a trendy expression of faith. Tragically, because Christianity for cool kids is still largely appealing to the consumptive desires of a high-ground world, it seems unlikely that churches who apply this strategy will meaningfully express and extend the shalom of God into the world. This too is a form of church that, like franchise church, is driven by appealing to the movers and shakers of society, albeit a different subset.

Ultimately, it would be hard to imagine a franchise church or a congregation of cool kids meaningfully expressing and extending God's shalom into the world, because it would be difficult to convince a consumptive community to embrace a costly way of life. If a church has high-ground DNA, it will seem nonsensical to vacate those spaces in favor of the low ground. It is more likely that churches who aspire to the high ground will stay that way in the long run.

We have an opportunity to honestly examine our life together and ask the hard questions needed to expose these tendencies at work in our church. If we don't, we will continue to drift toward a preference of high-ground folks over low-ground folks.

But I get *why* we do this, and I'm not even unsympathetic to the pressures that drive it. There's no denying the fact that ministry strategies centering on the movers and shakers are safer. They are is cleaner and neater. No mess, no chaos. People who have a lot of rough edges, who aren't clean and neat, who carry with them significant mess and chaos, often find themselves at the margins of, or are outright excluded from, our congregations. They just don't seem to be able to get their act together and assimilate into the cultural norms of the congregation.

Ministry to the movers and shakers is also strategically advantageous. There's no argument that ministry is hard, and sustaining the ministry of a church is even harder and getting harder every day. And it's certainly easier to sustain the current structures of the church if we center our vision on the enclaves of movers and shakers in our community, so it's tempting to design vision with those movers and shakers in mind. Trying to create expressions of church that would make high-ground folks increasingly comfortable and happy will, over time, tempt us to create subtle barriers to the low-ground folks because these are groups that do not congregate together in high-ground spaces.[4]

I don't think all is lost. We can start to make the kinds of changes to the way we create and cast vision that might open doors to new ways of being the church, which creates a new opportunity to express and extend God's shalom in and through the congregation. This is a critical conversation as we consider the future of evangelical expressions of the church because the vision of our churches cannot be centered on folks who live at the high ground and also be meaningfully engaged in the pursuit of God's shalom for those who occupy the low ground of our culture.

But to me, this entire conversation centers on this question: *Did Jesus come to the movers and shakers, or did he come to the moved and shaken?*[5]

You might say Jesus came for everyone. While that's true, I want to push that question a bit further and consider some key texts related to the way Jesus lived in the world and his vision for the kind of placement his people would choose in the world.

To start, let's reconsider Luke 4:14-21 again, where Jesus articulates that he is the one through whom the kingdom of God would take root in the world.

It's true that folks might hear the words of Jesus "I've come to preach good news *to the poor*" as an implicit exclusion, judgment, or critique. But if we can resist that impulse for a bit, we might be able to ask ourselves, What makes Jesus choose this text as a way of defining his ministry? I mean, there are likely countless Old Testament passages he could have turned to that would not have positioned the poor at the center of his ministry vision, so why did he choose this text? Given that Jesus didn't have to choose this passage, we should assume that he meant to choose it, and so we ought to take it seriously when we see that Jesus centered the poor and oppressed in his vision for his own ministry.

We might also consider again the vision of the sheep and the goats in Matthew 25. Jesus says, "Whatever you did for one of the least of these brothers and sisters of mine, you did for me" (v. 40). Again we see Jesus' concern is for the *least*, not all people generically but in particular the low-ground folks. We might find ourselves saying, "No Jesus, all lives matter, not just the least but also the most!" But Jesus seems intent to prefer the most vulnerable in his midst. Jesus calls these vulnerable ones his "brothers and sisters." In other words, Jesus is willing to see himself as family with folks who occupy the low ground of society.

This is the shalom community of God coming into focus. Jesus is inviting us to take note of the fact that he is creating a family with the most vulnerable at the center. When Jesus says "you did it for me," that should make us wonder if Jesus means to imply something significant about the quality of his presence among the poor and oppressed. It seems that Jesus is identifying with these low-ground folks to such a degree that he sees no discernible difference between himself and them. This makes sense when we consider the significant emptying and vacating of power, position, and privilege Jesus chose, opting instead to take up residence at the margins of society with those cast off by the movers and shakers. Indeed, his solidarity with the poor was so complete that he could be executed as a common criminal.

Jesus' focus on the low ground was so thoroughgoing that when Satan tried to tempt him in the desert, Satan appealed to the base human instinct to desire the high ground. Satan offered Jesus the chance to become a mover and shaker. Of course, the radical vision of Jesus was entirely other than the culturally acceptable pursuit of the high ground. Jesus chose not to make something of himself. He didn't take the form of an empire builder or a cool kid, but instead became a suffering servant. Jesus was utterly committed to life in solidarity with and for the sake of those who occupied the low ground. I often think about the song "Grace Like Rain" and the line "Hallelujah, grace like rain falls down on me." It's true that the love and grace of Jesus rain down everywhere and on everyone, but it is also true that it then gathers and pools up in the places in our society most vulnerable to the floods of poverty, brokenness, injustice, and death.[6] That is profoundly good news.

A STRATEGIC PLANNING FRAMEWORK

What do we say then about vision and strategy at the local church level? While I wouldn't want to prescribe something for every church in every time and space, what follows is a framework for articulating a concrete vision for what it means to be God's people in a particular time and space. It helps us center on the low ground of society in a way that honors the people who reside there, creates space for the shalom community to include both low-ground and high-ground folks, helps us embody the way of Jesus with intentionality, and makes the expression and extension of justice a more realistic possibility in and through a local body of believers.

This framework is not intended to be an all-encompassing ministry strategy but a way of creating the conditions for the long, slow work of cultivating concrete expressions of God's shalom in and through the congregation.

Returning to the text of Jeremiah 29—and remembering all that we noted earlier about Jeremiah's call to adopt a posture that is for the flourishing and transformation of the city—we can now ask, *What kind of concrete practices does Jeremiah offer that might help our church in our pursuit of God's shalom?* I've come to see two complementary sets of practices emerging from this text that help form the foundation of a ministry strategy serious about God's shalom.

Build and settle. The first set of practices emerges out of the beginning of God's message to the exiles in chapter 29.

> This is what the LORD Almighty, the God of Israel, says to all those I carried into exile from Jerusalem to Babylon: "Build houses and settle down; plant gardens and eat what they produce. Marry and have sons and daughters; find wives for your sons and give your daughters in marriage, so that they too may have sons and daughters. Increase in number there; do not decrease." (Jeremiah 29:4-6)

As we consider the work of the church in a neighborhood, we can first think of the work of building, which is a *creative* work. God is calling the people to *build, plant, marry, have children, and grandchildren.* These are all creative acts, the formation of something out of nothing, be it a house, a garden, a family, and so forth. This work of *building the world* and caring for what has been built (the people, the families, the fruit of the gardens, and the structures constructed) is an echo of the original call of God for Adam and Eve in the Garden of Eden.[7] Seen clearly, God commanded both Adam and

Eve, and these Israelites in exile, to the work of *creation*. In both cases they are plying the trade of image bearers to conceive of good things and to bring them to life.

Israel's location did nothing to change God's intention for them. Instead, God calls the people to recover their original vocation in Eden by applying it to the gardens of Babylon.

God calls Israel to *build*, but to do that work in a *settled* way. In this text we see God indicating that Israel will be in Babylon for a while, three generations and seventy years! They are not tasked with a short-term project. Instead, their *building* work is done with an eye toward generational permanence.[8] One might imagine Israel's work in this area as somewhat shoddy if they assumed it would not last or they were not there for the long haul. But God tells them from the beginning that they might as well *settle down* in the houses they build because their grandchildren are going to grow up in them too.

Because God's command to settle is given to a people in exile— that is, a people at the margins—we do well to hold these concepts in tension so we resist seeing this idea through the lens of a dominant culture that produces a destructive and unjust form of colonization. A people who live at the margins aren't capable of colonization, and so the posture of exile is essential for folks—particularly majority-culture folks—thinking through this framework in their context.

This notion of *settle* colors our conception of the creative work of God's people in a place because it forces us to grapple with the notion of a hyper-local, deeply rooted way of life. None of the work the people are tasked with can be done at a distance. Instead, there seems to be something innate in the charge that will force them to put down roots in a place for generations, to come to see the place as God does, a place worthy of God's shalom (which, of course, is what God intends the city to experience in the first place). What in our ministry vision has that kind of local and rooted commitment? What might change if we rejected all forms of commuter-community engagement where we drive into and out of communities of shattered shalom and instead took up residence in the very places most in need of God's shalom?

Also notice that the day-to-day work of being God's people in exile is really quite plain and unassuming. There is nothing particularly supernatural about the vocation of building houses, tending gardens, and raising families. And yet it is the first charge these exiles are given. Perhaps we miss something when we assume that the work of God's people in a place should be T-shirt-worthy work. These are not tasks that you make a celebration video about; they are ordinary human tasks that everyone does. I have come to believe this is exactly the point. This is a way of being the church that resists making the cultural high ground the center of its life. It rejects a franchise-church approach because it is concerned about the actual physical place (and the people that populate it). This is the essence of a parish approach to church. Its view does not extend beyond the borders of its own placed existence. This is not a small vision—it is a rooted vision—it is a radical commitment to channeling the energy and resources that might have gone to brand extension toward the cultivation of shalom for the place where they have put down roots and the people with whom they are called to fashion a common future.

This is also a way of thinking about being God's people that challenges the ethos of cool-kid Christianity because the entire work of rooting in place and doing the work of creation isn't an appeal to the cultural standard of cool. This is because Israel isn't called to build so that Babylon will accept them. They are exiles. They are considered the lowest rung of the ladder, people who live on the low ground of

Babylonian culture. They will never be relevant or trendsetters because they will always be other to the culture around them. So the creative work they are called to is for some other kind of purpose. God is calling the people to see a deeper kind of significance in an ordinary kind of life.

Seek peace and pray. Second, God calls Israel to a set of practices we can refer to as *seek peace and pray:* "Also, seek the peace and prosperity of the city to which I have carried you into exile. Pray to the LORD for it, because if it prospers, you too will prosper" (Jeremiah 29:7).

Thinking about this passage concretely, with an eye to the work of God's people in a place, something new emerges. If the work of building and settling could be framed as a *creative* work, then seeking peace and praying could be seen as a *re-creative* work. The very notion of seeking or pursuing the wholeness and flourishing of a place, of course, assumes that things are broken and out of whack. A merely *creative* approach would likely not satisfactorily address the brokenness in the lives of people and in the place itself. A more comprehensive strategy for the work of being God's people in a place then should include a layer of engaging the brokenness toward redemption and renewal. The same way *build and settle* engages God's original vocation for humanity, *seek peace and pray* is centered on God's future intention for all of creation. This is the central way of giving expression to God's tomorrow in a local place. To seek peace for a city and its inhabitants is to give people a picture of what God is doing in the world through Jesus. It's a straightforward way of leaning into the work of being the church in the world.

The work of seeking shalom is a way of seeing the place God has put us as a garden of God's intentions. If these sidewalks and intersections, and the people who walk along them every day, are a garden of God's intentions, then seeking shalom is like gardening: pulling weeds, caring for the most tender and vulnerable plants, and cultivating the entire garden to produce healthy fruit, an abundant harvest. This stresses the need to see ourselves as bound together with friends and neighbors because we are part of the garden as well. We might have a dual role—both gardener and plant—but we can never forget that we all are in need of shalom. It's a mutual work.

This passage is also a reminder that we do not simply go out to seek the peace of the city. We seek the peace of the city while being a people who pray for the city. Of course, I think that has a plain meaning application, pray for the place God has put us! Karl Barth said, "To clasp the hand of prayer is the beginning of an uprising against the disorder of the world."[9] We can't forget that God is at work and mysteriously works in and through the prayers of his people to bring shalom to bear in the world. Much would change about the work of God in local places if God's people were in earnest and consistent prayer for the place. (I can point you to the stories to support that claim.)

I also think "pray to the Lord for it" is a kind of posture statement as well. The work of justice can become relatively detached from a vibrant spiritual life with God. The work is hard, grueling, isolating, and discouraging, and so the cultivation of a healthy life with God can quickly fade. Jeremiah helps us see that the work of seeking the shalom of the place God has put us *requires* real dependence on God to do the work. We are reminded that we are not bringing the kingdom with us, but we are plying our vocation as God's people in a place—demonstrating God's tomorrow—*depending on God to see shalom bear fruit.*

The work of justice is not unspiritual or a-spiritual. Because the justice of God is about the kingdom of God taking root in a place, that means God's shalom *must* be spiritual and must resist devolving into a kind of partisan endeavor. We have to keep in mind that the primary enemy of God's shalom is not some opposition political party; it is a struggle against principalities and powers, the spiritual forces of darkness. I don't say this to obfuscate the tangible world effects of injustice and its perpetrators; rather, I emphasize this because, for every world leader who is called to account for their injustice, there are a dozen more waiting in the wings to exploit the weak and vulnerable. God's shalom coming to us in Jesus was a definitive moment in a cosmic battle. And we go into the work ill-equipped if we do it without a conscious and earnest dependence on God and a willingness to commit the fruit of our life together to God. We recognize that God is the one who ultimately brings the flourishing and transformation to people and places.

In the end, this strategic-planning framework puts flesh on the Great Commandment to love God and to love our neighbor as ourselves. In calling Israel to the creative and re-creative work of *build and settle—seek peace and pray*, God is calling them to demonstrate faithfulness to him as they love their neighbors. In this single way of seeing what it means to be the church, and how to go about being the church we are called to be, we are able to live into both sides of the Great Commandment at one time. The tangible suggestions here, and the suggestions that make up the bulk of parts two and three, are meant as pathways into mutual relationships with friends and neighbors with whom we share a sense of common story, the ones our futures are bound up with.

QUESTIONS FOR CONSIDERATION

1. What is the vision of your church? When you lay it over the notion of God's shalom justice and Jesus' overwhelming concern for folks on the low ground, how does it stack up?

2. How could the vision of your church make the moved and shaken central?

Build and Settle

1. What is your church creating in the world that reflects God's design and concern for the marginalized and often forgotten?

2. How are you developing an ethos of rooted presence (settling down) within your congregation? Is it stretching people to consider the generational impact in your neighborhood (rather than just their kids)?

Seek Peace and Pray

1. Name the brokenness of your community. How might God want to heal it? How might God position your church to be present in the midst of it?

2. Do you have practices that tie your presence in your community to God? How are you praying for the neighborhood? Are you authentically depending on God to bring fruit?

3. What would your church's strategic plan look like if it found its source in *build and settle* and *seek peace and pray*?

6

RECOVERING KINSHIP

HOSPITALITY AS RESISTANCE

Our food ministry was arguably one of the most successful ministries in the history of our church. It was an enormous food pantry. But rather than hand out prepackaged bags of food, the pantry space was arranged like a grocery store, and our neighbors shopped the aisles for food they wanted. When I first came on staff I was amazed at the thoughtful way the leaders of this ministry tried to make the experience of getting free food as human as possible. You could argue that the entire system of food pantries is flawed, but I witnessed incredibly compassionate people dedicated to creating a space that was caring, compassionate, and as equitable as possible within the limits of the existing paradigm.

One of the evidences of this was the fact that despite the culture of affluence in our congregation and the relative lack of crisis life situations among our people, folks who first encountered our church through the food pantry increasingly became part of our church. Over time the socioeconomic level of our church changed—for the better—because we were becoming much more stratified across the economic spectrum.

However, as a pastor, this created a problem for me. At the beginning of the food ministry, the decision was made to refer to folks who visited the pantry as guests. Today, we might cringe at that language, but when the ministry was created it was an attempt to intentionally pivot off of language that turned people into charity cases. In church gatherings we regularly told stories of our "guests" and the way God was at work in this ministry.

But now these guests were increasingly joining our church. They were sitting next to me in the pew. For a while, I didn't recognize what I was doing, continuing to call these folks "guests." But over time, I recognized that we had a relational barrier in the church, and I was actively reinforcing it. We had food pantry "guests" and "regular" folks in the same room on Sunday morning trying to be a single community. It felt like a gut punch when I thought about what it must feel like to be called a "guest" in the church you call home.

There was no *we* here. There was *us and them*. It was an unnatural kind of community that had unintentionally—and with good motivations—erected walls that prevented mutuality and friendship between those providing a service and those receiving it. We wanted to be a family but were working against ourselves. We were missing an incredible opportunity—the chance to recover an experience of transforming kinship.

God has always been at work drawing a community deeper into his shalom community. God (Father, Son, and Spirit), a people (but deeper than that even), a family. God is an expression of eternal, unshakeable, incorruptible kinship.

It is amazing to me that God would desire to share that kinship with us, and that the purpose of the creative work of God is to give us a taste of the kinship God has feasted on throughout eternity. That the redemptive work of God—the reformation of a people— would be toward the end of overcoming the sin and brokenness that corrupted and incapacitated our participation in the kinship of God leaves me awestruck. God is renewing and restoring us, a refashioning of our person and of God's people, into a community fit for the shalom community of God.

KINSHIP

On my relatively short list of spiritual heroes, Father Greg Boyle is near the top. Father Greg has spent decades working with gang members in Los Angeles. Over that time he has helped give shape to the largest gang prevention and reentry work in the world. Most compellingly, it isn't a project to him. It's a work of family. Father Greg observes, "I suspect that if kinship was our goal, we would no longer be promoting justice, we would, in fact, be celebrating it."[1] This statement saturates the ethos of the community in formation at Homeboy Industries in downtown LA.

If there is an idea I believe more deeply than these words from Father Greg, I have yet to discover them. Like putting a guitar back in tune, his statement realigns my heart with God's in a profound way. Father Greg connects the dots between my convictions regarding the local church and my convictions regarding justice.

There are many who might bristle at or even categorically reject Father Greg's assertion. But we need to wrestle deeply with these thoughts because the evangelical impulse toward issues of injustice, particularly when it deals with the character of our relationships, has been to gloss over the long history of slight, injury, discrimination, and outright oppression. These injustices have shaped our national story as well as the story of the church in America, and we have not done the hard work of wrestling with the implications of that long history of hurt.

Considering how tone deaf we can be, Father Greg's idea might feel unsatisfactory for folks who have experienced the pain of injustice at the hands of their brothers and sisters. This is a reaction

I can appreciate and is one for which I have deep compassion. But Father Greg is not advocating a kind of blind acceptance of the past or just moving on from the wounds of history and the relational infidelity we (those from positions of power and privilege) have perpetrated against the most vulnerable people in our midst.

Father Greg often quotes Mother Teresa, who said, "If we have no peace, it is because we have forgotten that we belong to each other."[2] This sentiment makes sense through the lenses we have examined thus far. God, eternally existing in a perfect kind of kinship as the Trinity, created us for that same perfect kind of kinship shared between God and humanity. We were created to live in an eternal shalom community. From the beginning we have belonged to one another as we have together belonged to God. That is our human story, and more significantly that is our story as the people of God.

Belonging to one another does not erase the serious history of injustice that has invaded our experience and destroyed the shalom community of God. It does not mean that the record of the grievous action of high-ground folks toward low-ground folks goes away if we join multicolored hands in stadiums full of people and pray. Instead, the reality that we belong to one another, and have always belonged to one another, serves to *increase* the shame of the injustice and deepens the bruises of our collective experience of oppression, marginalization, and exclusion. It is true that we belong together, *and* it is true that men have systematically dominated women, white society has categorically oppressed people of color, rich communities have exploited poor communities, and so on. That we belong to one another only highlights the extreme unfaithfulness of these actions throughout history. It is a more egregious reality, in my mind, that this is our story in light of the fact that God had purposed that we should live in shalom community together.

The answer to the kind of soft reconciliation peddled within evangelicalism today is not the rejection of reconciliation but a rejection of the impulse to excuse behavior through the language of reconciliation, which is not the same thing at all.

A few years ago I attended a gathering of community-development and justice practitioners, and one evening conversations turned to the issue of race and reconciliation. One white brother suggested that since Jesus had come and the cross meant sins are forgiven, confession and lament related to racial injustice were not needed and were, in a way, antigospel because they made white folks feel shame (something the Scriptures suggest we ought not experience anymore). The next morning, the tension felt toward this guy was palpable, and he and I found ourselves in a fairly intense conversation related to why this line of reasoning was unhelpful.

He was engaging in a way of talking about the work of the gospel that sought to excuse the national story of injustice and overlooked the cultural and systematic ways that we continue to abide with racial injustice in the church. He was a prototypical apologist for "let's just hold hands, sing, and get over it." Even though he was using the language of reconciliation, he had no imagination to understand the work of reconciliation.

But I think we can—and need to—speak of reconciliation because, theologically speaking, it's an accurate frame of reality. That reality should increase—not numb—our sensitivity to the gross infidelity to the shalom community perpetrated against people at the margins over centuries. Those folks who represent groups (men, white, rich, etc.) who have historically acted unjustly toward marginalized people need to learn how to be in this kind of community, recognizing that we come to the work of building relationships fit for the shalom community at a significant relational deficit. This must shape the way we consider the work of building community within the church, specifically within the local church.

We belong to one another. The presence of injustice evidences the fact that we *have* forgotten that and *continue* to forget that. To be a people who are both just themselves and are able to do justice in the world, we need to see the work of pursuing kinship with one another and with folks on the margins (low ground) as essential, ongoing work as we seek to live into the fullness of what it means to be God's people.

If we hope to cultivate communities of God's shalom, we need this notion of kinship more than we need almost anything else. But we also need a way to get there. Saying that we are aiming for kinship is all well and good, but if we don't have a sense of where we are now and how we might move toward kinship, we will spin our wheels in frustration.

KINSHIP AND THE SHALOM COMMUNITY OF GOD

Father Greg highlights the reality of kinship over and against its contradictions:

> Inching ourselves closer to creating a community of kinship such that God might recognize it. Soon we imagine, with God, this circle of compassion. Then we imagine no one standing outside of that circle, moving ourselves closer to the margins so that the margins themselves will be erased. We stand there with those whose dignity has been denied. We locate ourselves with the poor and the powerless and the voiceless. At the edges, we join the easily despised and the readily left out. We stand with the demonized so that the demonizing will stop. We situate ourselves right next to the disposable so that the day will come when we stop throwing people away.[3]

On the one hand we have kinship, and on the other we have the outsider, the marginalized, those denied dignity, the poor, the powerless, the voiceless, the despised, the left out, the demonized and disposable. When we consider the reality of our world, we see a lot more of these things than we do the reality of kinship. We also see the way kinship really is the experience of justice in community. There is no soft peddling of reconciliation being discussed here. Instead, kinship is the fruit of a community committed to relational righteousness in ways that include not just personal actions and motivations but also engage the systemic and cultural issues that war against the shalom community of God. *Justice* and *kinship* are essentially—in the eschatological and ecclesiological sense—synonyms. For churches committed to justice, a focus on the cultivation of kinship within community is essential work.

So what is the role of the church related to those who do not experience kinship? What does the reality of exclusion mean for local communities of faith that desire to give expression to God's shalom in the world? What's more, how do we face ourselves honestly and confess the extent to which our congregations function to extend margins more than shalom?

Kinship cannot exist where margins are tolerated, where dignity is overlooked, and the folks on the low ground of society are told to stay where they belong. If in our way of being the church we are not vigilant against the subtle movements of exclusion that codify systems of marginalization, we will struggle to extend God's shalom into the world in meaningful ways. On the other hand, local congregations committed to cultivating a way of being in community together that unearths these dynamics and struggles against them in favor of the pursuit of kinship are well positioned to embody the intentions of God in a world hell-bent on stratifying people groups for the purpose of exclusion.

OTHERING AND THE BODY OF CHRIST

Community developer Julia Dinsmore calls this kind of cultural exclusion "othering," and this dynamic is a powerful carcinogen accelerating the illnesses plaguing the body of Christ today.[4] "Othering" describes the *actions* of people that work to highlight the difference in someone else or that reveal a deep blindness to the way we wield our cultural sameness to the exclusion of those who occupy a different cultural story. We do this all the time in evangelical spaces, and not always in ways we might initially consider unjust.

For example, in the late 1980s through the 1990s, evangelicalism experienced an explosion of growth through a wave of church planting and the momentous rise of the megachurch movement. The growth of both of these movements is attributable in no small way to the work of Donald McGavran and Peter Wagner and the formalizing of what they called the Homogenous Unit Principle (HUP). Their 1990 book *Understanding Church Growth* laid a philosophical foundation for evangelical leaders who envisioned a fresh way of organizing church.[5] The basic thrust of their work argues that sociologically, people are more comfortable interacting with people who are like them, and from the perspective of the church they are more willing to congregate, associate, and participate in a faith community if the others with them mirror their various cultural identities. By organizing church around sameness of any kind, a church could remove a number of "obstacles" that create personal, internal resistance to congregational affiliation. When you extend that argument, the HUP cosigns the notion that conversion is easier through the removal of the barriers of cultural difference. To put in the positive, in a space of cultural sameness a church can expedite the process of a person turning their life over to Jesus.

The impact of the HUP in evangelicalism is thoroughgoing. Beyond the well-documented examples of massive megachurches who attribute their growth to the fastidious application of the principles of the church-growth movement, an overwhelmingly high percentage of what we do in the church is organized around the HUP, particularly in efforts related to outreach, evangelism, and church growth and planting.

HUP—perhaps unintentionally—trains us in the church to prioritize the comfort that comes with cultural sameness. So, the way we organize our day-to-day church life works to mitigate any sense of discomfort in our ministry spaces. Consider the developments in youth and children's ministry over the last twenty to thirty years. One priority of most churches is to develop the capacity to hire staff to run ministry for youth and children, and to do so in a way that gathers them together in spaces of homogeneity. (I have worked with churches who hire youth pastors before lead pastors because this desire is so strong.) In the entire history of the church, it is a very recent development that children and youth would be shepherded and nurtured by the church in spaces compartmentalized from their parents. But nearly every church I have encountered has a deep desire to do just this. And with good motivations, I believe. Accompanying that desire is an understanding of the nuances of child and youth development and a commitment to the faith formation of young people that are properly adjusted for those insights.

At the same time, the rise in compartmentalized ministries for youth and children has created a pattern of behavior that insulates adults and young people from one another's cultural differences. In the main, we are quite used to the expressions of worship, teaching, or church activities that have developed over the time of this separation. We know how *we* do things and clearly recognize the differences in the way ministry is done for children, for youth, for adults. These differences are often accepted because of the separated spaces the groups usually inhabit in church. But what about when these worlds collide?

In both churches I served as a pastor, one of the most consistent issues of conflict came over the clash of culture between youth and adults. At no point was this more on display than when we attempted to worship together. These combined worship services, though rare, created more tension and frustration within the congregations than almost anything else we did. For weeks leading up to the gathering, staff would stew and fret about making the time palatable for both groups.

How will we make sure the kids aren't bored?

How do we control the kids so the adults are not annoyed?

I hope you can hear in these questions an overriding concern for comfort. While comfort and sameness are not conscious values in these situations, they are the dominant ones. We experienced such a sharp decline in participation in these gatherings that we consistently had to question doing them because "people just don't want to experience worship this way." The disruption of our comfortable patterns of being in this church space were more than we were willing to bear, and these were with our own kids! In absolutely every instance, everyone breathed a collective sigh of relief when this experiment in relative heterogeneity was over and we could essentially retreat back into our sameness.

The great tragedy is that the effect of our homogeneous ministry model guards the sameness of each cultural group vigilantly, even against the other groups within the whole. Over time the model, adopted to expedite and aid the work of the church, actually serves to create hairline fractures that splinter when we disrupt the cultural norms of HUP in practice.

Christena Cleveland notes that this way of creating *minimal groups*, "groups that are formed based on an inconsequential characteristic" in the hope of helping lessen the complexity of our larger groups, "actually serve[s] to create unhelpful categorical boundaries between different groups." To describe this dynamic, she employs the language of "in-group" and "out-group." An unintended result is that "simply putting people into groups . . . increases the likelihood that [people] will focus on the specific factor that divides them . . . and disregard the more significant factors that unite them," and that "the distinctions that separate one group from another are guarded at all costs."[6] She demonstrates the way these seemingly inconsequential groupings deteriorate into mechanisms for the valuation of people (those not a part of the group are deemed as less important) and codifies the boundary markers of division between groups.

Cleveland gives us language to describe why our congregational culture had so much trouble creating space for youth and adults to worship together. The seemingly meaningless distinction (made for reasons that conceivably could have merit) had started to deteriorate into an us-versus-them dynamic.

This is also what was happening in our food pantry. A subtle, nonmalicious line had been drawn between church folks and food-pantry folks, and the physical integration did nothing to overcome the divide. The food pantry folks didn't fit the pattern of our congregational profile, not because we didn't want them to be part of the family—we did!—but because something else was getting in the way. This is a nearly unavoidable result of HUP's application in our church life.

HUP AS IMPLICIT EXCLUSION

When applied to day-to-day ministry, HUP seeks to clearly define the way we differentiate people from one another under the auspices of nuancing our ministry approach for the benefit of each group. While I would not want to suggest that the results of this have been entirely bad or to say there is no space for thoughtful and critically evaluated application of HUP, an overriding effect of its application in the American evangelical church has been a culture of implicit exclusion.

Since HUP demands the definition of a target group of folks sharing a common cultural trait, it also functions to exclude those who do not share that same trait. As the evangelical church has grown away from a parish model of ministry, which attempts to define a ministry target by geographic boundary—theoretically, although in reality never, detached from cultural characteristics—the result has been a widespread practice of predetermining the type of person our ministry is designed for. This means that, by virtue of defining an in-group based largely on common cultural traits, our ministry strategies overwhelmingly function as mechanisms that exclude the "other." In other words, othering is easy in the church.

And if this is easy to do between kids and their parents, *imagine how easy it is to do across racial, gender, and class lines.* When we lay out the long history of injustice and its toleration—or proliferation—in the church, we can see the effects of othering. Sometimes it is intentional, often it is not, but it is rampant. Unless we are willing to engage our blind spots in this area, particularly within the white evangelical context, it is likely we will continue to perpetuate injustice. We won't cultivate communities of God's shalom. The dream of a church that *is* just will remain a dream.

HOMOGENEOUS UNITS AND THE IDOL OF COMMUNITY

This is a massive problem for the church. As long as we are content to predetermine the type of people we desire in our community, we will create something far less than church. In fact, we may well be creating communities of idolatry. In his book *Life Together*, Dietrich Bonhoeffer explores this notion of creating an idol out of community and the ultimately destructive work it does to the church. He says,

> Those who love their dream of a Christian community more than they love the Christian community itself become destroyers of that Christian community even though their personal intentions may be ever so honest, earnest and sacrificial. God hates this wishful dreaming because it makes the dreamer proud and pretentious. Those who dream of this idolized community demand that it be fulfilled by God, by others and by themselves.[7]

Usually we apply this idea to individual people and the way we tend to prioritize our preference when it comes to our personal participation in church. But isn't the pervasive application of HUP in the American evangelical church an outworking of the same kind of idolatry? The predetermination and preferencing of particular kinds of people are as clear a way of falling prey to Bonhoeffer's critique as any other. It creates an ideal community shaped by a commitment to being comfortable, and we lose the essence of the body of Christ when we do this. What makes it particularly dangerous, though, is that we do so for theoretically sanctified reasons and without a mechanism to check our inner pride and pretension because we are convinced of its "missiological" benefit. In the end, I find myself hoping that we haven't fashioned a bronze-bull version of the people of God, which ends up leaving us in a perpetual state of ecclesiological idolatry.

OUR WELL-WORN PATHS OF EXCLUSION

I suppose it shouldn't come as a shock to any of us that something as seemingly innocent as a missiological strategy could have such exclusionary results. The entire history of our nation has relied on the powers of exclusion to define the fault lines between people groups and reinforce the position of those who occupy the cultural high ground. The narratives of race, gender, and class in this nation are rooted in the reality of exclusion and othering. Othering and the exclusion it creates are part of the air we breathe as humans and certainly as Americans. It shouldn't surprise us when we see it creeping into the church as well.

What's more, when I survey the story of my own life I see just how easy it is to fall into the patterns of othering and exclusion. Growing up largely unaware of the dynamics at play in our society, I naturally fell into the well-worn paths of exclusion that frame day-to-day life in our society and our churches. And even to this day, as deeply engaged in the work of justice as I am, full of head knowledge related to the injustice of othering and exclusion, I notice that my defaults are still programmed by the rules of the exclusionary game.

It takes a significant amount of work to break out of the ruts of sameness and to create meaningful spaces in our lives for those who are a kind of cultural other. The principles undergirding HUP are true in the sense that engaging in meaningful relationships across any line of difference takes more intentionality, humility, and energy than relationships that exist within a sphere of sameness. Building relationships that resist the cultural forces of othering and exclusion requires a kind of discipline that, at least, I am not accustomed to needing in order to develop friendships. So I find that when I'm tired, stressed, wounded or emotionally thin, I retreat back to sameness, back to the well-worn paths of exclusion.

It is a short distance between recognizing the extra work of intentionality required to engage relationally and resisting and resenting the people with whom relationship requires more of me. Perhaps you've noticed this in your life.

But once we accept the basic moral neutrality of continuing to opt for the comfort of sameness in our relationships, we become unable to resist the forces of exclusion our preference for cultural sameness sets in motion. The same way our embrace of high-ground forms of church undercuts our capacity for justice, so too our willingness to exclude and other people across lines of difference resists kinship and seriously impairs any effort to lean into the vision of the church as a people who live in and out of God's shalom.

If our default mode as humans in community is to engage in othering, how can we resist that while reshaping our way of life to embrace an honest kind of kinship?

XENOS AND THE PRACTICE OF HOSPITALITY

Ana Maria Pineda's wonderful chapter on the practice of hospitality is one of the finest explorations of the great possibility that comes with recovering this vital Christian practice.[8] The authentic practice of Christian hospitality is a direct response to the reality of othering in the church today.

Pineda centers her discussion of hospitality on the Greek word *xenos*. In the New Testament, *xenos* is used both in the sense of "stranger" and "guest"—wherever we encounter one of the words, we are encountering the other. In the mind of the New Testament

Christian, they are interchangeable. To think of a stranger (one who is other or strange to our way of being) is to also think of a guest. Pineda argues that "this one word signals the essential mutuality that is at the heart of hospitality."[9]

This interplay between *stranger* and *guest* reinforces the notion that the intention of God includes an ever-widening circle of people who experience the shalom community of God. And this movement of stranger to guest is needed to start to overcome the exclusion and othering that happens in our lives and in our congregations.

At the same time, this stranger-to-guest notion is quite foreign to us. The line that God draws from stranger to guest is not a part of our natural way of thinking. Instead, we are taught to see the stranger as a threat. There are countless ways we interrupt the journey of stranger to guest. In the main, strangers never become guests—to say nothing of friends and family. We need to be able to identify what is interrupting the movement from stranger to guest.

The interruption of the movement of *xenos* is *xenophobia*. Xenophobia is the injection of phobia—fear—into the liminal space between stranger and guest. Fear severs the line between the worlds of those two words. When fear is allowed to run free, *xenos* is corrupted and becomes *xenophobia*. When we give into the fears produced when we encounter the stranger, we likely find ourselves engaged in othering.

If we think about examples of othering, we see how clearly phobias have corrupted our capacity to embrace the true sense of *xenos*. When a presidential candidate refers to all Mexicans as rapists and then calls for a wall between our border and theirs, we see, quite literally, the capacity fear has to put up walls between groups. When we encounter someone of a different race on the street and put a protective hand over our wallets or purses, we see the way fear undercuts a moment for real human connection. When we consider the extra-intentionality a party at our house would take if we invited all kinds of different folks from different cultural groups, and so opt instead to just invite people we are comfortable around, we see how even a threat to my temporary comfort and momentary emotional state might cause us to erect a wall between ourselves and the other.

We can't make meaningful progress in the recovery of authentic kinship in our churches until we are able to authentically unearth, name, and examine the fears that drive this othering. These fears are ruining any chance we have at deepening our engagement in the shalom community of God.

This is where the corporate spiritual discipline of hospitality comes in. If *xenos* is the goal and *xenophobia* is a corruption of our ability to live into that New Testament vision, hospitality is a way of resisting our fears and creating a new space not governed by othering.

Hospitality, in the New Testament, is the word *xenophilia*. If the movement of stranger to guest is corrupted by the introduction of fear, then the response required to resist fear is *philia* or love. Hospitality is the Christian practice of demonstrating love of stranger and doing so in a way that evidences our willingness to be in community (stranger to guest) with them.

Some might suggest the practice of hospitality is still fraught with all kinds of unhelpful power dynamics (host-guest, etc.). It's possible to corrupt hospitality in this way, but the truest sense of the Christian practice of hospitality is pure and full of virtue. To become the kind of people who can create space in which strangers—folks the world teaches us to fear—are welcomed is radically prophetic work.

I am not using the term *welcome* in the sense that they must always come to us. Instead, this notion of *welcome* is a kind of relational posture. My friends do not have to cross any relational barriers to be friends with me. They are *welcome* with me as they are. On the other hand, a person I don't know has barriers to cross to be friends with me. Because of that, they are less *welcome* with me—not because of any ill intent—but because of the barriers present that impede our relationship (lack of trust, shared story, etc.).

The practice of hospitality is how we unearth our othering tendencies and create the possibility of a new kind of community. At its basest form, hospitality is a way of being that creates a low-barrier space of welcome for anyone encountered. It is a way of life that refuses to create divisions that impede relationship and each person's participation in the community. This requires more work, a willingness to be inconvenienced, disturbed, disrupted, made uncomfortable, stretched, and spent for those it would be easier to distrust and exclude.

HOSPITALITY IN ACTION

Hospitality is often framed as a practice or discipline for individuals. That is, we ask individual believers to be hospitable, to diversify their tables, to show kindness to strangers, and so forth. It will always include that of course. But the assumption that individuals committed to radical hospitality on their own will shape the corporate ethos of a congregation is a bad one. Instead, if we commit to the work of developing a communal character to our hospitality, we can then disciple individual people in our congregations to discern the implications of our corporate commitment to hospitality for their lives.

We need to start with a vision for communal practices of hospitality. And we begin to gain this kind of vision when we recall what hospitality truly is, a rejection of fear of the other through concrete practices of love. Julia Dinsmore says, "Whenever we notice 'othering' going on, we have to interrupt that."[10] These are the marching orders for a local church seeking to flesh out what hospitality looks like in their community.

Where are people being othered and how can we interrupt that? Notice, the first step in the practice of hospitality is learning to recognize othering. I remember a conversation with a friend who is a church planter in a wealthy suburban city. As he surveyed his community he could not discern the "injustice" he could help his congregation engage. However, as we started thinking through this notion of othering, he quickly identified the local Muslim community as an excluded, thus othered, community. So the question moved to *How might his local congregation interrupt the othering they were seeing?*

Interrupting othering is a two-layered move. The first move deals with the lived experience of being othered. Henri Nouwen is helpful here as he notes that the practices of hospitality give shape to a life that allows us to "convert the *hostis* into a *hospes,* the enemy into a guest and . . . create the free and fearless space where brotherhood and sisterhood can be formed and fully experienced."[11] The first thing we see here is the essential connection between genuine hospitality and mutuality. This is not a stilted version of well-mannered power dynamics. Instead, hospitality is about creating the spaces for authentic and mutual kinship. Second, Nouwen's comparison of the hospitable space and the hostile space is interesting. It points to the reality that hostility is synonymous with othering. In other words, the lived experience of being othered is the experience of hostility. Interrupting othering involves the creation of a safe space for those experiencing hostility.

After the 2016 election, many immigrants in my neighborhood experienced the hostility brought on by the rejuvenation of nationalist and racist themes by the president elect. That rejuvenation resulted in physical assault and violence in our community directed at these immigrant populations. As a response, a local group, prompted by many in the Christian community, began a campaign of yard signs that said, "Hate has no home here." These signs gained rapid attention and have spread across the nation as a signal that the hostility directed at the other will not be tolerated. Obviously, these signs do not in and of themselves create a safe space in the face of violence (counting the number of signs in the neighborhood could be a vanity metric, after all), but as a metaphor they are helpful for this kind of work. The church has an opportunity to recognize the hostility toward others and cultivate creative expressions of God's intention that hate and hostility are not at home here. The real work of this is finding concrete ways of creating safe spaces so that people who are being othered can experience something new and different.

The second layer that interrupts othering is to recapture the stranger-to-guest dynamic. Instead of allowing fear to corrupt *xenos*, we can interrupt that by engaging in the work of stranger-to-guest hospitality. This is work that can flow in both directions. As my friend discovered the exclusion experienced by the local Muslim community, his church began looking for ways to pursue some kind of intentional relationship with the local mosque. Surprisingly, the mosque invited them to come for a lunch where everyone could get to know one another a bit more. This experience began to open new doors of possibility for this congregation to live in the world in a different way. In the end, the stranger-to-guest dynamic is reclaimed through the sharing of stories, and the cultivation of a shared story. This is how any relationship builds, of course, which is much more important when the relationship is tenuous and threatened by the many layers of difference that existed between these two groups of people.

This is a pastoral work. It is difficult for anyone to be exposed to their own othering tendencies. When we name that dynamic at play within our church, we must be aware that we are not only calling people to see plainly their own sinful brokenness, but we are also bringing a relational schism to light. This will include seeing the way the young and old are treated in relation to those between eighteen and sixty. Or women compared to men. Minority groups to majority groups. Poor in relation to the rich. This could go on and on. As we think through these dynamics and evaluate the extent of our own exclusion, it becomes incumbent on the pastors and leaders to guide a congregation in the naming and interrupting of these othering tendencies.

PASTORING THE PARISH AS RESISTANCE

You could argue that the answer to the problem of the homogeneous unit is the heterogeneous congregation. I totally agree. Over the last decade and a half, congregations have increasingly sought to do just that. Over that time, though, folks have started to ask questions about the approach. *Does an intentional vision for diversity work to reinforce whiteness by pressuring people of color to assimilate?* Studies suggest it does. *What happens in these congregations when cultural difference arises, and might it work to further exclude minority groups within the congregation?* Studies reinforce this as well. *What about congregations in homogeneous contexts? Do they need to leave their context and recruit difference?* This is a common counterpoint to the charge that the multiethnic church is the clearest picture of God's reconciling intention.

This is a critical conversation, and I often find myself split down the middle on these issues. I've begun to wonder though if these are still problems because we see diversity as a solution but we've failed to name the real problem. Until we move past our allegiance to the homogeneous unit even our attempts to diversify will still trend homogeneous. I'd wager this is at least part of the reason why the increase in multiethnic evangelical churches happens in upwardly mobile contexts because the target group isn't specifically tied to race but rather class. In other words, it's trying to find *xenos* from the high ground.

What if, when we think about hospitality and the recovery of authentic kinship, we started by asking, How do we resist the impulse toward the homogeneous unit principle? How might we do that? Again, I think we might look at pastoring the parish as a way of actively resisting HUP.

Recovering a deep sense of parish is evidenced by a commitment to rooting out othering in our lives, noticing and resisting othering in our parish, and standing alongside those being othered. This could open us up to transformative work both in us and through us. It might also allow us to ask the question about diversity in new ways. What I'm describing is a *low-ground* approach to creating a sense of family within our way of life together that's more at home crossing lines of cultural division, be it gender, race, class. Father Greg reminds us of what happens when we do this. We discover we are "inching ourselves closer to creating a community of kinship such that God might recognize it. Soon we imagine, with God, this circle of compassion. Then we imagine no one standing outside of that circle, moving ourselves closer to the margins so that the margins themselves will be erased."[12]

QUESTIONS FOR CONSIDERATION

1. Who is being othered and excluded? Even within our normal congregational life?

2. How might we interrupt that by creating safe spaces to experience relationship and life without hostility?

3. How can we cultivate a safe space to share our stories and develop a sense of shared story?

7

FINDING COMMON
KINGDOM GROUND

DISCIPLING PEOPLE INTO SHALOM COMMUNITY

When the young man heard this, he went
away sad, because he had great wealth.

MATTHEW 19:22

HIGH-GROUND DISCIPLES

When Jesus instructed a young man to sell his possessions and give it all to the poor, the man went away sad (Matthew 19:16-22). This young man is a prototype for a high-ground person. Youthful, rich, and convinced of his status (often referred to as a ruler, signaling power and influence as well), he came to Jesus looking for confirmation that he was worthy of eternal life. In his mind, these markers of social status were irrelevant to the question of religious fidelity; he thought his rabid attention to the law was enough.

That shouldn't surprise us, because the high ground traffics in merit-based assessments. There's no blaming this guy: rabid attention to performance is how high-ground folks are trained to measure their success, so why not religious faithfulness? It also makes sense because high-ground people are usually deemed worthy when measured against the cultural markers of merit. In nearly every arena of life, high ground folks are measured and consistently found acceptable, successful, and exemplary. Positive performance is a primary barometer of worth. For this young man, religious excellence was a reflection of the status he had achieved (or inherited) in every other area of his life, but it was also a nod to the unwitting assumption that social factors did not have a bearing on his faithfulness. Religious perfection could be pursued divorced from the rest of life.

Jesus cuts through this notion and informs our perspective on discipleship for the congregation committed to the pursuit of justice in the world. In Jesus' view, this young man's social location was a *primary* factor of faithfulness, a reality we often overlook. But this reality slowly sunk in for this man as he came to grips with the fact that Jesus was calling him to a kind of discipleship foreign to a high-ground world. The things that got him to the top were liabilities that had to be proactively dealt with for him to achieve "perfection" in Jesus' eyes.

Jesus says it is easier for a camel to go through the eye of a needle than for a rich man to enter the kingdom of heaven. The disciples respond with a sense of hopelessness, "Who then can be saved?" (Matthew 19:25). They recognize the impossibility of the kingdom of God integrating into the high-ground world of the upwardly mobile. At this point in the story, nearly everyone is despondent. Nobody thinks it's possible for this guy to follow the call of Jesus. Only Jesus sees a way forward, saying, "With man this is impossible, but with God all things are possible" (v. 26). What is normally used in a generically spiritualized way (something high-ground exegetes are want to do), this declaration that all things are possible with God is strikingly specific. Jesus says that in the world's terms it is impossible for high-ground people to be faithful in the kingdom of heaven. But this kind of work is not impossible with God. Consider Nicodemus, a high-ground person because of his academic achievements and cultural authority. Jesus not only confuses him (cutting against his intellectual prowess) but also uses the image of becoming a baby *again*, which, for a powerful man, would have cut to the core.

By a stunning work of God, both of these men can divest themselves of the riches of power and privilege and become the kind of people who can follow Jesus deeply into the life of light and liberation.

It seems Jesus is saying that a high-ground person cannot faithfully follow Jesus without a radical transformation of their high-ground reality. (By extension a high-ground church will find itself similarly positioned.) This is radical, challenging, and uncomfortable. It engages emotions no one (including me!) who lives on the social high ground is particularly comfortable with. But if we were to take Jesus at his word, this might be worth exploring rather than rejecting because on the backside of that emptying is the kingdom of heaven. A worthy prize, no?

Alternatively, when we consider the way Jesus interacted with folks at the margins, the poor, lame, sick, and demon possessed, the flavor of those conversations took a very different tone. When Jesus encounters the vulnerable and marginalized, we see the depth of his compassion and the gospel expressed through freedom and new life. The social location of low-ground folks played a major role in the way they hear, receive, and respond to the gospel as well.

A church committed to justice will ensure that a person's social location is woven into their discipleship framework *because* social location shapes the way people hear, receive, and respond to the gospel. If we hope to cultivate a just way of life together in the local church, we should take seriously the notion that we must evangelize and disciple people in a way that takes their social location into account, even as we balance that with the goal of forming a family of faith in which each person is seen, honored, and valued.

This stands in contrast to many of the main strategies for discipleship and evangelism in the evangelical church at large, where we would find little to no discussion of the impact of a person's social location on the way we proclaim the gospel to them and on their process of discipleship. For the sake of mass production, our discipleship and evangelism tools are largely one-size-fits-all. In a typical high-ground evangelical congregation, a person's social location is usually value neutral. Wealth, race, culture, gender, power, education, influence, and so on, are factors often off-limits to the questions of discipleship. Like the rich young man from Matthew 19, generally we are more comfortable with discipleship that excludes social location from the conversation.

Yet even a cursory reading of the life of Jesus leaves us with substantial evidence that we have seriously missed the boat as it relates to how a person's social reality influences the path of discipleship. The Scriptures give us example after example where Jesus makes the characteristics of a person's social location central to the vision he casts for their faithful discipleship. While the gospel story of what God is doing in the world through Jesus is a single story, the way we hear, receive, and respond to that story is significantly impacted by where we stand when we encounter it. If we want to cultivate congregations that reflect the shalom community of God, then we would do well to reclaim this nuanced approach to discipleship. It might seem daunting, even impossible, but again, take Jesus at his word: "With God all things are possible."

THE WAY OF JESUS IS THE WAY OF
DEATH AND RESURRECTION

Eric Law's wonderful book *The Wolf Shall Dwell with the Lamb* outlines a vision for multicultural spirituality and leadership. In it he suggests that one way of thinking about spirituality, or in our case discipleship, is being caught up in a rhythm of death and resurrection.[1] Remembering that the story of Jesus is one of both death and resurrection, and remembering the countless times Jesus calls disciples to take up the cross *and* find new life in him, Law suggests that giving people vision for both in a regular rhythm of discipleship is helpful. This is important because, as Law makes clear, life in the kingdom is the goal for everyone. We are calling every person to be part of the shalom community of God, participating in a people who are giving expression to God's justice in the world. It is a single call. But individual people enter that story in different places.

Emptying at the high ground. For high-ground folks, we can offer an invitation—an ongoing invitation, not a single conversion moment—to daily life in the kingdom that reflects the movement of Jesus highlighted in Philippians 2:5-8:

> In your relationships with one another, have the same mindset as Christ Jesus:
>
> Who, being in very nature God,
>> did not consider equality with God something to be
>> used to his own advantage;
> rather, he made himself nothing
>> by taking the very nature of a servant,
>> being made in human likeness.
> And being found in appearance as a man,
>> he humbled himself

by becoming obedient to death—
even death on a cross!

Jesus, like the rich young man, was also a prototype for a high-ground person. But unlike the rich young man, Jesus divested of the riches and privileges of heaven and came to earth occupying the low ground alongside the most vulnerable and marginal among us. Jesus—setting the example of divestment and a serious change in social location—then calls people like the rich young man, Nicodemus, and countless others to emulate his posture in the world. He said things like "Whoever wants to be my disciple must deny themselves and take up their cross and follow me. For whoever wants to save their life will lose it, but whoever loses their life for me will find it. What good will it be for someone to gain the whole world, yet forfeit their soul?" (Matthew 16:24-26).

Jesus is taking direct aim at the high-ground folks listening in. After all, doesn't the world of the upwardly mobile prioritize accumulation and consumption such that self-denial would be a radically important virtue? Isn't the high ground a social space that values safety and self-preservation such that the notion of losing one's life would sound scandalous? It seems Jesus was serious when he called high-ground folks to emulate the way he modeled; he calls them to let go of the very things they have been "finding their life" in.

Unfortunately, these are the kinds of passages we tend to turn into abstract notions of measured generosity or serving others. Jesus is inviting those who, *like him*, find themselves in positions of relative power, influence, wealth, and so on, to, *like him*, empty themselves of the privilege these things have afforded them. To the extent that these passages are not taken as straightforward invitations from Jesus, we can be sure that our framework for discipleship and evangelism is muting the impact of a person's social location on their formation and discipleship.

Because our social location differs from person to person, there is no formula for what this looks like. This is not one-size-fits-all. Instead, the pastoral work of discipling folks at the high ground comes in (1) helping people hear the call of Jesus to join him in a different social location, (2) shepherding people as they discern those things that they have used to define themselves (their worth, status, etc.), and (3) create proactive and tangible ways of self-emptying that do not reinforce the division and adulation of the high ground over the low ground.

In practice, it seems that we too often allow people to find their life without first losing the things they've been using to make a life for themselves thus far. If the life of Jesus is exemplary for us in this, it invites us to see that it is impossible for an intentionally upwardly mobile person to follow a downwardly descending Jesus unless they are willing to change course—repent—and imitate Jesus' self-emptying in tactile ways. The life of Jesus helps to frame the reason we call people to this because in his life we are reminded that we can only experience resurrection from the low ground.

Lifting up as low-ground discipleship. Turning again to Philippians 2, Paul says,

> Therefore God exalted [Jesus] to the highest place
>   and gave him the name that is above every name,
> that at the name of Jesus every knee should bow,
>   in heaven and on earth and under the earth,
> and every tongue acknowledge that Jesus Christ is Lord,
>   to the glory of God the Father. (vv. 9-11)

There is, of course, much to be said about this passage, but we can note that in order to experience God lifting him up (exaltation) to new life and glory, Jesus had to take up residence on the low ground. He does not stay there though; he then experiences the resurrection power of God from that social location.

Seen in that way, we can again look at the concrete moments of Jesus' life when he encountered persons on the low ground (e.g., the woman at the well) and see that since they inhabited that particular social location, they were already positioned to experience the resurrection power of God. They needed to be lifted up, and their social location was the *only* factor we can observe that made it so. Think about Jesus drawing the attention of the disciples to the poor woman who gave out of her poverty (Luke 21:1-4), Jesus *lifted her up* in the midst of the community even though she would not have measured up by any high-ground standard. Had the high-ground man who followed her simply matched her gift, his contribution would have been seen as insufficient.

The Gospels relate story after story of ways a person's social location affects the way they hear, receive, and respond to the gospel. Jesus is the same, the story of what God is doing in the world through Jesus (the gospel) is the same, but we encounter it differently and are called into it daily through different postures and experiences, depending on where we stand when we encounter the story.

Excluding social location from our discipleship makes it hard to faithfully grapple with the injustice perpetuated by the division between the high ground and low ground of our society. A church that can faithfully express and extend God's justice in the world must be able to do this. One of the primary ways we can lean into this work is by taking seriously this notion that our social location affects our discipleship and to call people into the gospel rhythm of emptying and exaltation, death to self, and resurrection life.

For churches that are primarily made up of high-ground folks, this means that we will have to narrate the gospel and the path of discipleship the same way Jesus did for those folks. We must be willing to engage the social location of the upwardly mobile and invite them to empty themselves in order to faithfully follow *the way* of Jesus. Not doing this is selling a false bill of goods, a gospel devoid of some of the essential postures required for living it out. It reinforces a way of thinking about faithful discipleship that would allow people to believe that simply following rules to perfection is how we demonstrate faithfulness, something upwardly mobile folks would be eager to hear. The rich young ruler had fallen into the false gospel of religious performance that excluded his social location. We are selling that false gospel when we pretend the gospel is one-size-fits-all. Instead, there is a bigger, better, and more beautiful gospel and way of life that comes through emptying ourselves, because it is from the low ground that we taste the resurrection power of God.

How are we inviting high-ground folks to empty themselves to take up residence in low-ground spaces? If we cannot answer this question tangibly, I submit that communities of kinship will always stand at arm's length from us. However, when high-ground folks take the way of Jesus seriously enough to divest and take up residence in community with folks who occupy the low ground, serious discipleship has taken place and a community of kinship is now possible.

For pastors in high-ground contexts, how does your discipleship strategy address this dynamic? Do your people hear and receive the gospel of self emptying? If not, it's possible that you have wrested the gospel and the way of Jesus from the place where Jesus centered it, out of a person's actual concrete social location. Reconsidering our discipleship strategies to take this into account is a vital move for churches who want to more faithfully give expression to God's shalom.

For churches that are primarily made up of low-ground folks, though, it is a mistake to call people into emptying first because, socially speaking (economics, power, influence, etc.), they are already empty. In a community wracked by generations of poverty, the call to give up everything falls on deaf ears. Poverty is the root cause of so many social ills, and to voluntarily submit to the very thing that has destroyed a person's community is unconscionable. In this case the gospel of resurrection power, of new life and new creation, invites the people of a vulnerable community to "taste and see" that the Lord is good. Not in an American consumeristic way of thinking about prosperity but—through the lens of Jeremiah 29—we are calling people to follow the way of Jesus that leads to flourishing, transformation, and abundance.

In these contexts are we preaching a gospel of resurrection, new life, flourishing, and transformation that resists American consumerism, or have we uncritically enmeshed our theology of resurrection with a vision of American upward mobility that confuses the social high ground with the kingdom of God? This is also a bait-and-switch gospel because we cannot tell people that the high ground is what God wants for them only to turn around and call them into the rhythm of self-emptying. Indeed, churches who fall prey to confusing resurrection with the social high ground forsake the essential message of Jesus to high-ground folks and attempt to allow newly minted high-ground people to feel quite blessed in their new social location. In the end, we find ourselves in the exact same place, preaching a gospel that disconnects faithful discipleship and our social location. The great tragedy of this is that social factors are directly connected to injustice and so when we exclude those factors from the process of discipleship we render our church impotent to address the very things that drive injustice in the world.

Ted and Mike often sat together in a three-month intensive job and life-skill development course we ran through our church's nonprofit. These two guys couldn't have been more different. Ted was a CFO with a healthy family and stable housing, and was a significant part of our leadership team at church. Mike's life had essentially fallen apart. He had no stable income, no network of support to speak of, and had fallen into a pattern of homelessness that was tinged with a note of hopelessness and cynicism. They were a real odd couple.

Part of our job-training strategy included having community gatherings outside of class where we could intentionally resist our personal temptations to see ourselves as service providers and hopefully build a sense of family together. Mike showed up at all of these nights. We shared food and laughter together. He chatted with my kids and engaged in prayer and Bible study time. Mike was a devout atheist, always quick to point out the logical fallacies of my faith. But he kept showing up.

Ted couldn't come to these nights, but he could do other things. Ted put his social capital on the line. He set up lunch after lunch with Mike and his own business contacts. They worked together on crafting a résumé and how to network. Ted leveraged his reputation and resources for Mike's benefit. And this is no small thing. It was risky and cost him to do it. Ted would go on to do this for other folks in the class in ways that demonstrated his embrace of the call of Jesus to divest himself from his high-ground position.

Which person was being discipled here? The path was different, but they were both responding to the same gospel. The discipleship culture at this moment held together the tension of a community with high-ground and low-ground folks. Ted was hearing the gospel's call to emulate the downward way of Jesus, which he did again and again. Praise God! Mike was hearing the gospel too. But to him it sounded like welcome and community in a life experience with plenty of places where he might have felt shame. Praise God! Our discipleship patterns have to hold this together, because folks on the high ground need a different way of coming to the kingdom space than folks on the low ground.

In either case, we can't forget that discipleship involves a *rhythm* of death to self and resurrection. The story of Jesus includes both, and our stories include both. Each of us gets caught up in a way of life that involves self-emptying, taking up the cross, and dying to self, only to then experience the profound and mysterious new life of God waiting for us in the depths of our self-emptying. As we live in and around this rhythm we all, high ground and low ground alike, find ourselves on new ground, the ground of the kingdom of God. We got to this new space precisely because our original social location mattered, not because it was left out of the equation from the start.

So when we ask people to own their social location (acknowledge its reality), we don't mirror the world's approach, which seeks to keep a person securely in that space. Instead, acknowledging our social location is a starting point from which we carve out a way of life in community where people can move from where they stand into a rhythm of death and resurrection.

In this kind of space the gospel of radical grace takes on new life. Irrespective of our track record of success or failure or our perceived benefit to the body, we all find ourselves swept up in a story which teaches us that the things we use to define ourselves or define others by do not determine our place in the shalom community of God. Instead, those factors become the baseline for understanding what it takes to become an evermore faithful part of the community giving expression to God's shalom in the world where nothing is missing and nothing is broken. This is grace, not *despite* my social location but *from* my social location. I am *even still* invited into this community where I come to know the one who calls me to die and invites me to experience new life.

In this community of shalom, where the love and grace of God in Christ are lived out, I am not excluded because of my poverty; nor am I exalted because of my wealth. This is one of the ways that our communities begin to take on the character strong enough to resist othering in all its forms. It allows us to put a low-ground vision into practice in a way that doesn't judge the poor or ultimately exclude the upwardly mobile. Sound impossible? I suppose from a human perspective it is, but . . .

TAKING THE TEMPERATURE OF YOUR DISCIPLESHIP

As a One on the Enneagram, I am faced with a daily battle against my innate need to be perfect. I'm not a perfectionist that agonizes over every little detail of an assignment. I'm more of a moral perfectionist. I don't have to get every answer right, I have to *be* right. I have an overactive guilt complex that runs a narrative loop in my brain telling me I'm not good enough; I don't have value because I don't have enough virtue.

My Enneagram One-ness is the reason I resonate so deeply with the story of the prodigal son (or the lost sons). I feel deeply the shame of the younger son who, after coming to his senses, starts the return journey to his father like it's an exercise of self-flagellation. *I'm not worthy to be his son. I've messed up too much, offended too deeply, made too many mistakes. I'm not a son—I'll be a slave. I'll sleep in the barn.* I know that kind of shame all too well.

I also resonate with the older son, who is outraged by his father's seeming disregard for his young brother's lack of moral virtue. *I've been keeping all the rules, and what do I get? He's a total screw up. Why does he get rewarded for that?*

As disparate as the experiences of both brothers are and how widely their responses seem to differ, they are actually falling prey to the same ugly lie. They both believe *merit* is what determines their father's favor. The younger son thinks he doesn't have enough merit to be accepted and loved, and the older brother agrees. And the older brother thinks he has done all he needs to warrant feeling worthy, but he doesn't get the response he desires. As tragic as this story is in so many ways, it's heartbreaking that both brothers labor and toil under the strain of thinking their performance determines their standing in the family.

This is the gospel of merit, the bootstrap theology that is all too prevalent in the evangelical world. Though we may preach a gospel of grace alone, we often practice a gospel of merit. People's status, station, and success establish the place they occupy within the family of God. The longer I pastor and participate in the local church, the more convinced I am that this is an incredibly pervasive belief for Christians. We don't intentionally become the older brother; we become the older brother because we are scared to death that we don't merit the favor of God.

When we look for ways to demonstrate our worth, the temptation is to highlight our value at the expense of the "less deserving." This is the Pharisee in Luke 18 thanking God that he was not like other people—those sinners—who are less worthy. This fuels the othering that corrupts kinship. It destroys our capacity to be family with folks who occupy different social ground. If we don't start rooting out the gospel of merit, it will be difficult to disciple a congregation *from their social location* to the common space of the kingdom of God.

It might prove fruitful to take the temperature of discipleship in your congregation. As you unearth the hidden belief patterns, you may be able to discern the extent to which the gospel has been conflated with merit. The gospel cannot thrive in a meritocracy and, not surprisingly, neither can justice. Resisting the cultural forces of performance and merit, and the cultural narratives of shame that accompany falling short, will require intentional, regular, and pro-longed effort in preaching, counseling, discipleship strategies, and leadership development.

In spite of the hard work, the fruit of a more nuanced vision for discipleship that takes social location seriously in the process of formation is possible. Jesus says so anyway. Let's try it!

Even in the quest to cultivate a communal identity for a people—rooted in a parish—seeking God's shalom, we need to examine the way we are moving individuals who make up the community into this shared identity. One-size-fits-all discipleship will not suffice if we hope to see God's justice bear fruit in and through our community. Having a nuanced strategy for the discipling of individual people—which considers social location as essential to the path of formation—will make or break our pursuit of the shalom community.

QUESTIONS FOR CONSIDERATION

1. Is there room in your discipleship pathway for nuance and differentiation for people from different social locations?

2. How will you invite people into a process of naming social location as an important factor in discipleship in a world where no one wants to bring up that topic?

3. Are there concrete ways you are connecting discipleship and obedience to justice? If not, how do you take steps to help people see that justice is inextricably connected to personal and corporate faithfulness?

8

WORSHIP

QUESTIONS THAT DRIVE HOW WE GATHER

"I wanna know if you become the pastor here, will a person like me be welcome?"

Larry's question stunned the congregation gathered for my first candidating weekend in Brooklyn. Larry's life was in total chaos. He suffered from pretty severe mental illness, had endured years of abuse from his family, and was subjected to multiple occasions of forced institutionalization for episodes when he acted out in ways that frightened onlookers. He had even caused physical harm in a particularly scary violent outburst. Larry had found his way into the care of some of the folks of the church and began showing up for services on Sunday—I think, initially, as a way of escaping situations on the street. But over time, he found a modicum of acceptance from this little band of believers. His question struck us all as a sacred-ground moment. We were deeply aware of just how important it was and that his question was challenging us to confess and realign our corporate life with the radical welcome of Jesus.

But it hadn't been easy. Larry's mess and chaos were impossible to ignore. During and after church services he would go on rants and tirades that were unnerving at best and would often have to be talked down from whatever had triggered him. So his question was no small ask from a congregation that had dealt with him a lot over the couple of years leading up to my arrival. After I arrived, Larry made his presence known every week by walking in late, and while I preached from the floor at the front row, he would walk slowly down the middle aisle to the second row—standing just a couple of feet from me as I attempted to preach—and take his seat front and center. One day, after he came in late, he fumbled around with his offering money (a plastic baggie full of loose change), and proceeded to drop it, slowly, all over the hardwood floor of the sanctuary. It was not quiet.

There were days when it would have been easier to simply tell Larry to leave. Days when a lot of tension would have been released had we just asked him to find somewhere else to go on Sunday mornings. There were seasons when we asked him to take a break—after some heightened tirade had crossed the lines of safety—but it was never an exclusion. We made all kinds of spaces for Larry to stay in community with us while he rehabilitated a bit and got back to a place where he could participate in a healthier manner. As a congregation, we wrestled and wrestled with Larry's place in our community and what it meant to be a place where he was in fact welcome.

Did we get it right? I know we didn't. But I was proud to be a part of a congregation that tried so hard, so often, to work out what it meant to be a people where folks at the margins felt an authentic sense of belonging.

The truth is that Larry's presence in our community made us better because he regularly shattered our illusions that we were anything other than a people in process. Any impression we might have had that we were a well-oiled machine capable of handling anything and everything that came our way was disabused by Larry's consistent meltdowns. Our Sunday gatherings were anything but polished, and Larry's interruptions were both evidence of our corporate imperfections and an insurance policy against us ever perfecting our Sunday worship.

I came to relish his place in our pews on Sunday because he made it possible to say what was true, that we were an imperfect people. Larry was no more imperfect than me, and I no better than he. Society suggests that I am better because I have more socially acceptable issues, which is a damnable lie that I buy into more than I care to admit. I think Larry made us a more human congregation because we were forced to acknowledge our limitations in a way that so much of modern church culture is organized around hiding.

Evangelical congregations are fond of saying that they are cool with people's mess. We talk about messy faith and that it's okay to not have it all together. We project an image of safety for people to bring their struggles, imperfect stories, and crises into the community of the people of God and to find that they—like Larry—are welcomed. I think we really want to want this. It has not been my experience, though, that this is really true.

Corporate worship gatherings are often the last place a person could go within evangelical church life and find it okay to not be okay. We are pretty uncomfortable with mess. We don't usually know what to do with someone whose life is in shambles or chaos. The Larrys of the world function as interruptions to our agenda, particularly in the corporate worship gathering. There is not a lot of space—cultural, relational, physical, or temporal—for people to work out their mess in the light of Jesus and his kingdom when we gather together for worship. I obviously can't speak for every church in every place, but my experience (in my entire life growing up in white evangelical spaces) is that what we do in worship often doesn't feel human enough to reach down into real human experience, specifically the experience of pain, brokenness, or the underside of societal norms. We want to be places that welcome everyone from everywhere, but when we gather together our normative patterns seem to resist creating an authentically hospitable space for people at the margins.

I wonder if part of the reason is that so many corporate worship experiences try to emphasize the wholly other nature of God in a way that lifts people out of their day-to-day experiences. We turn down the lights and close our eyes. We sing songs that are totally weighted on the side of a transcendent God—marked by an over-saturation of abstracted spiritual notions and metaphors—in an attempt to draw people into an encounter with God that is powerful and meaningful. More aggressive forms of this will channel extra energies into aesthetic choices in the worship space, fog machines and laser lights, for example, that are aimed at elevating people beyond the world, where the things of earth might grow strangely dim, for an hour or so on a Sunday morning.

There is a difference, though, between a manufactured experience and a genuine encounter with the God of Abraham, Isaac, and Jacob. I will confess my nervousness that, in the name of transcendent spiritual encounter, we often settle for a manufactured worship experience that leaves us little room for a genuinely human encounter with God. It seems there is a correlation between the degree to which the corporate worship experience has a manufactured nature and the extent to which a veneer of propriety and respectability is preserved.

In Brooklyn we had to choose between the veneer of propriety and respectability our worship gathering projected and Larry. In a congregation as small as ours, there was no way around that decision. But it isn't always the Larrys that force us to make those kinds of decisions. Corporate worship is always going to be a reflection of the culture of the congregation. When people engage in corporate worship, they are picking up clues—some subtle, some not so much—as to who this space was created for, who is authentically welcome to be here. If the pursuit of God's shalom in the world depends on the local congregation becoming a particular type of people in the world, then it would be foolish to overlook the implications of our corporate gatherings for the work of justice. Recovering a more whole and human vision for corporate worship is essential for congregations dedicated to cultivating communities of God's shalom. We don't need to reject the wholly other nature of God to engage the concrete realities of our shared human experience in worship. But if we aren't intentionally cultivating language and practices that weave those things together, we will likely continue to prefer an abstracted and manufactured worship experience.

RESISTING ABSTRACTION IN WORSHIP

For example, *would someone who only lived in your sanctuary know that there is a real world outside of it and that that world is wracked with injustice?* If we were to consider the normative experience in many evangelical churches, it would appear that the real world outside the walls of the church was not considered. Ignoring the world outside, particularly the moments of extreme brokenness and injustice, is a subtle way of being a high-ground church. Because high-ground society is largely insulated from the injustice of the world, there is a certain degree of freedom not to talk about issues that arise in our world. For people who experience life as vulnerable or marginalized people, walking into a gathering for corporate worship and *not talking* about the issues they experience day to day often seems offensive.

I am persuaded of the deep connection between the production of an abstracted worship experience and the lack of meaningful welcome experienced by folks who come from backgrounds—or are dealing with life seasons—that don't match the cultural DNA of the congregation.

Over a series of weeks, a zealous, justice-minded member of my church introduced me to several families she had invited. I was excited to see if they might find a home in our congregation, but none of the families ever returned. I followed up with our church member, and she said they all liked the gathering, but it was clear to them they didn't belong. They felt, even though there were explicit messages of welcome, from me and others, that the implicit message of exclusion was being projected throughout our gatherings. It probably doesn't surprise you to learn that all these families were black and had experienced worship in our mainly white congregation as intimidating or marginalizing. We hadn't done anything overtly antagonistic, but under the surface the message was clear that they would not find a home in our congregation. I suspect it came down to the fact that they experienced a fairly abstract worship gathering that matched the cultural sensibilities of white evangelicals but that had little to do with their lived experience.

Why this disconnect? Because many churches project the belief that social location is irrelevant; it belies the belief that our lived experience *gets in the way* of worshiping God. These churches might talk about our lives as obstacles to God or proclaim that God loves us *in spite* of our experience and circumstance. Contrast this with the worship traditions of people of color, where a person's and a people's lived experience is often the *source and fuel* for the worship of God. In these traditions, God does not love us *in spite of* our circumstances but rather *in the midst of* our experience. This is a *huge* paradigm shift for mainly white evangelical churches. But it is a shift we must make if we are to disciple a people toward justice. We cannot engage meaningfully in the work of seeking God's shalom in our way of life together if we de facto ignore the realities of injustice when we gather together for worship. To ignore the injustice of the world will make our vision of justice hazy as we demonstrate the kingdom.

Churches seriously committed to God's shalom justice will naturally integrate the realities of the world within their corporate gatherings. Easily, the most natural place to begin doing this work is through prayer and preaching. If your gatherings have space for communal prayer, then there is already tilled soil for the prayerful consideration of the events of the day and the impact those events have on friends and neighbors and other members of the shalom community. Preaching gives us a way to look at the events of the day through the lens of what it means to be the church and the vision of the kingdom of God. While I don't consider preaching to be primarily didactic or educational, I do think that sustained and thoughtful, not just episodic and reactionary, preaching on the themes of shalom, justice, eschatology, and ecclesiology will hone our shared vision for the desires God might have for our life together in community and in a community.

MOVING PAST PLEASANTVILLE

While we seek to integrate the concrete realities of injustice in our corporate gatherings, we must also be committed to honoring the full range of human emotions within our life together. We are not always great at creating space in corporate worship for the wide spectrum of emotions that people experience in life. Many times, the best we can do is to acknowledge that *it may have been a hard week, but we are here to praise the Lord!* Of course, the implicit message is that we have to leave the pain or bitterness of our experience at the door in worship. Often, it seems like we prefer happiness over the experience of every other emotion. I can see why we do that and can affirm the reality of deep and abiding joy that marks the follower of Jesus. I suspect, though, that it is not always that deep and abiding joy we are trying to draw out of people, but a reflection of our own sense of discomfort with the painful experiences of life. I've pastored countless Christians who simply don't give pain and sadness room in their life, authentically offering it to God in the hope of redemption. Instead, folks often push those experiences down and attempt to *conjure* a sense of joy because that feels like what is expected of them when they walk in the doors. In this way, the manufacturing of corporate experience and the personal suppression of every expression save *smiling* work hand in hand. Sunday morning feels a little too much like *Pleasantville* to be truthful to the human experience.

This is one of the primary ways we reinforce the message that our congregations are not safe for people who experience the daily trauma of poverty or folks who have tasted the bitter fruit of injustice in the world. If we hide behind a veneer of *happy*, we will struggle to cultivate a community where people experiencing the pain of injustice can authentically share their experience in community. On the other hand, when we find ways in our gatherings to regularly and explicitly create space to name and honor the full spectrum of our emotions and experience while giving God room to work in our midst, we actively resist the temptation to manufacture an experience that works to exclude folks at the margins. These are communities where each individual member finds the welcoming space needed to authentically bring their entire self into community and worship.

RECOVERING A VISION FOR CONFESSION AND LAMENT

A regular rhythm of prayers of confession and lament gives us even more fertile soil for the roots of justice to deepen in our community.

Having both confession and lament allows a congregation of high-ground and low-ground folks to stand together in one another's lived experiences and carry those burdens at the same time.

When I think of corporate confession, I come back to the images of Isaiah 6. Isaiah, ushered into the throne room of God, sees the Lord and immediately turns to confession: "'Woe to me!' I cried. 'I am ruined! For I am a man of unclean lips, and I live among a people of unclean lips, and my eyes have seen the King, the Lord Almighty'" (v. 5).

An authentic encounter with the Lord is a straightforward invitation to confession. This runs counter to our demonstrated way of thinking that an authentic encounter with God looks like abstract disengagement. Instead, genuinely coming into the presence of God drives us squarely into the dirt and dust of our everyday lives through the invitation to confession. It is a difficult prospect to invite people into a regular rhythm of confession. Yet Isaiah's experience ought to be our own. Before Isaiah can enthusiastically say, "Here am I. Send me!"—something we love to talk about in missional evangelical spaces—he must first honestly say, "Woe is me."

Beyond this, Isaiah's encounter with the Lord brings not only his sin but also the sin of his people into full relief. Isaiah's confession is corporate; he stands willing to take on the sins of his people before the Lord. This is *the hardest part* of corporate confession, specifically for high-ground folks. Used to being lauded for personal achievement, the notion that I would shoulder the guilt of others or see myself as guilty by proxy is a foreign concept. Particularly in congregational climates where grace is cheaply thrown around to mean that we need not ever reckon with our ongoing sin and brokenness, calling a people to serious communal confession is difficult.

Yet, in our day, when we see such incredible injustice fueled by issues of systemic racism and socioeconomic oppression, this is an essential element in the formation of a people who can give expression to God's shalom in their midst. Distancing ourselves from the sins of our people is a nuanced version of othering that maintains a sense of innocence in the face of violence and oppression. For us to be in meaningful community across the spectrum of social divides, corporate confession with an eye to confessing sins of injustice is a hard road, but it's one we must begin to walk.

At the personal level, the regular practice of confession disciples us toward the kingdom ground where high and low ground come together and can form authentic kinship. In Luke 18, Jesus tells the parable of the Pharisee and the tax collector. Both have come to the temple to pray, and the Pharisee stands and prays, "God, I thank you that I am not like other people—robbers, evildoers, adulterers—or even like this tax collector" (v. 11), while the tax collector "beat his breast and said, 'God, have mercy on me, a sinner'" (v. 13). It's interesting to note that, depending on your perspective, either man could be seen as the high-ground or low-ground person in the story. The lack of clarity is instructive. When we gather for worship in a community that represents people having come to the kingdom space from their respective social locations, we will be tempted to set ourselves apart from the other. We will naturally look for ways to delineate our differences in a manner that elevates our sense of worth and standing before God. Jesus points us to the posture of the tax collector because it is the act of confession that resists the *othering* being perpetuated by the Pharisee. Confession invites us to see ourselves on equal footing with others, in need of the redemption of God. In a worshiping community that creates meaningful space for confession, we cultivate the possibility of God's shalom.

The practice of lament also calls a community into alignment with God and one another in the face of injustice. Over the last few years we have watched young black men murdered in extrajudicial killings splashed across our TV screens. For brothers and sisters in the African American community, these stories, while not new, have taken on a new level of intensity. Tragically, white brothers and sisters have often disregarded this pain and excused this injustice out of ignorance or indifference. So, while predominately black churches have had occasion after terrible occasion to lament these experiences, predominately white congregations have barely noticed. For a congregation seriously committed to justice, this cannot be. The same way we create space for confession, we must also create space for lament. Lament must be specific. It must not only name the pain but also the injustice that caused it while calling on God to make right what is wrong in the world.

For too long we have not shared these laments together. Creating space for lament in the liturgy of your church gives you an opportunity to bring different communities together in one voice. Lament is the prayer language of the low ground.[1] When we invite high-ground folks to lament, we are not excusing the injustice perpetrated. Nor does it excuse the need for confession by folks whose people enacted the pain. Instead, inviting everyone to join together in lament is an invitation to join together in a shared story, to release our judgment and indifference, and to straightforwardly experience the painful experience of another like it was our own. Lament is essential to the life of a just church because, as Soong-Chan Rah reminds us, "Shalom requires lament."[2]

Having both confession and lament as regular rhythms in our liturgy not only gives voice to the lived experience for everyone in our community, it also invites us to hold these polar experiences in our life together as well. Ultimately, this is how we continue to resist othering toward a radically hospitable space in our lives. If we are discipling people to be able to hold the pain (lament) and sin (confession) of others' stories in shared community, we are moving well into our identity as God's people committed to justice.

WHAT STORIES ARE WE MAKING CENTRAL?

A third question to help shape our liturgy is: *What narratives are we making central in our gatherings?* Let's consider this question at three levels.

First, oftentimes the storytellers in a congregation are the leaders or pastors. This is normal and not always bad; indeed, it is necessary. However, in many cases, they are the *only* people who speak publicly in a congregation and so they shape the narratives. In this case, the stories "from the bottom" are never told and never heard. I've been in more than one meeting where the notion of giving the mic to the congregation makes everyone's spine tingle. I understand the nervousness related to opening things up for people to contribute to the story of the worship gathering, and I've heard all the arguments for why controlling access is important. However, the more we control access (or the more doggedly we screen out certain types of people), the more we are in danger of projecting the clean, eloquent, and "appropriate" voices. This is a way we manufacture our worship into something that is less than human.

There are simple things we can inject into the liturgy that might open up possibilities over time. At the church I was a member of in Chicago, we dedicated serious time *every week* to sharing pain and celebrations publicly, widely, and without screening. Sure there are the occasions when someone "eats the mic" and talks forever, but even if that is a bad thing—and I'm not sure it is—creating that regular space has also given rise to some of the most powerful moments of storytelling and celebration I have been a part of. These moments would have been missed if the mic stayed in the hands of the sanctioned leaders.

Additionally, the greeting time in many churches is often surface level and a bit perfunctory. Is there a way to infuse intentionality into the greeting time—and I don't mean use it to change the set on the platform—that would allow corporate gatherings to be more of a work of the people? Beyond that, in many churches we put fences around things I'm not convinced we have to fence. I understand that many theological streams might want to make sure the person presiding over the Lord's Table is ordained, but otherwise, what kind of intentional moves can be made to ensure that we are all telling the story of what God is doing in the world through Jesus together? These are immediate changes we can make to give shape to our liturgy. They will help us make sure we aren't centering on the narratives of people in high-ground positions and that the story being told by the decisions we make about *who really matters* within the congregation is a reflection of the whole people of God.

Second, we ought to consider the theological narratives we center on. This is a huge conversation related to issues of race, gender, and culture, and who is writing the theology we consider normal versus theology we consider to be from a cultural, racial, and gendered perspective. Without engaging that entire dialogue now, we can specifically address the stories we tell in our gatherings— particularly in predominately white spaces. Are the theologians we quote and illustrations we give from one cultural, racial, or socioeconomic group? More specifically, when do we make central the narratives of people from nonwhite, nonaffluent, and nonmale groups? My hunch is that for many evangelical congregations, we may try to tell different stories, but we might only do that when talking about issues that make sense to hear about from someone of that group. We might talk about racism and quote a black theologian, but do we quote a black theologian when we are preaching our way through Luke? That might be more rare.

The more we reinforce the stereotype that we can only hear from diverse voices when the topic centers on "their issues," the more we actually reinforce the divides we are trying to overcome. The theological narratives we make central shape our community and reinforce which voices seem important and trustworthy. Creating a culture in our congregational life together that can hear and celebrate the voices of every part of the body has to resist centering on the high-ground narratives from a theological perspective.

Third, we can apply that same sensibility to the question of what cultural and historical narratives are central in our congregational life. We have a tendency to engage national, cultural, and historical narratives that favor the experience of one group of folks over others in our congregation. For example, evangelicals have somewhat uncritically embraced major national, patriotic holidays as moments when we highlight religious freedom within our liturgy. This integration of "God Bless America" with corporate worship is a fairly straightforward version of civic syncretism. The presence of Americana in our worship is a clear-cut expression of idolatry we have in the church in the United States (but that is another book or at least another discussion). Americana worship also centers the experience of those who have lived in the majority and dominant position in American history.

When we thank God for the freedom we've experienced in this country without even thinking to ask how people, whose story is something quite a bit less than free, experience that notion of "freedom," we give evidence of our blindness in the way we focus on the largely Anglo-European narrative in our corporate worship. For African American and indigenous people, celebrating "freedom" on the Sunday nearest to July 4 is a far different experience, one that might be painful and oppressive. Our inability or unwillingness to resist the celebration of Americana in our worship will dramatically impede our capacity to engage instances of injustice with confession and lament. We will be culturally too committed to the national narrative to see, confess, and lament national sins. There is no way to cultivate a community that exhibits the shalom of God between disparate groups of people if we continue to make a white American cultural narrative central to the way we worship.

So, instead of blindly making an Americana narrative central in our worship, we can nuance our approach to give voice to the myriad ways that people and people groups have experienced—and continue to experience—our shared story in this nation. That is already something we do in minor ways. I've noticed that on days that are somewhat given to sentimentality in our churches (Mother's Day, for example), many churches have started to nuance their way of engagement. There is a sense of joy and celebration, but churches have also started to create space for those who experience a holiday like that in a decidedly different and especially painful way. To that end, we have the imaginative space already in many congregations for us to resist the blind celebration of a shallow version of freedom or civic religion that is indifferent to the experience of the historically marginalized and oppressed.

There is no reason we could not create space for, say, an immigrant to celebrate the fact that they came to the United States in pursuit of certain things, and has experienced a more whole and healthy life here, and then also lament together the ways indigenous people have experienced incredible injustice at the hands of European invaders. These are tensions we will find ourselves in if we take this path. This is not easy ground to tread, and it might not be the first step in the process. But it is possible to advocate for intentionally resisting overt displays of Americana that engages the diverse experiences of people in the midst of the national narrative.

Corporate worship gatherings are too important to overlook the subtle ways we undermine our own attempts to cultivate communities where God's shalom can take root and bear fruit. These spaces can foster shalom community (not as the only focus, of course) while doing the whole work of the church in its liturgy. My hope is that we find ways to do that without making every other topic take a back seat. Rather, as we are going, we find ourselves in an ever-deepening shalom community with the language to confess and lament injustice and with a broadening ability to celebrate voices and stories from the historic and cultural margins. Authentically just worship will do those things naturally and gives us concrete ways to grow into God's vision for the people of God.

PART 3
WHAT'S NEXT?

9

POWER

A CONVERSATION ABOUT THE LINCHPIN OF JUSTICE WITH JULIET LIU AND BRANDON GREEN

Power is a tricky concept. It's a moving target, hard to define, and easy to abuse. It is always real but sometimes intangible. Some of us carry the trappings of power and privilege everywhere we go but are unable to see it. Some of us experience its ugly effects because we rub shoulders with people blind or indifferent to the damage they inflict with it. If our churches are going to faithfully participate in the work of extending God's justice into the world, we will have to wrestle with the issue of power. Particularly considering the relative silence of the evangelical church on the way power works to solidify systems, just or unjust, it is critical to examine our use of power through the lens of what it means to be the church seeking to cultivate God's shalom.

A CONVERSATION ON POWER IN THE CHURCH

Juliet Liu and Brandon Green have been friends and colaborers in ministry for several years. In addition to being the editorial director for Missio Alliance, Juliet serves as copastor at Life on the Vine Christian Community in Long Grove, Illinois. Brandon serves as both associate pastor at River City Community Church in Chicago and the partnerships director for RCITY CDC, the church's community development nonprofit.

These are two leaders I've come to trust as we grappled with ministry issues together. I seriously respect their pastoral wisdom, sharp theological minds, and passion for God's justice taking root in their local communities. It seemed obvious for us to wrestle with the nature of power and the church. We also want to model how to engage the issue of power in community and to discern together—in writing—what it means for the church to take this issue seriously.

ADAM: Thanks for taking time to reflect on these questions and give your insight to this project, Juliet and Brandon. I'd love to begin at a kind of personal level. *What comes to mind when you think about power in the church?*

I see a lot of people who have power try to get away from it. They either ignore it or pretend they don't have power. I may be a bit of a nerd here, but this reminds me a lot of how Frodo responds when he discovers the true power of the ring in *The Fellowship of the Ring.* He freaks out! Tries to hide it so no one will find it. I've interacted with leaders who have incredible amounts of power—because of their inherent characteristics (e.g., white, male) and because of a tangible position of authority in the church—who react like Frodo. These leaders chafed at (in fact, they got mad at me) for bringing up the fact that they had power. It made them nervous and uncomfortable. Does that ring true for you?

JULIET: In my church context, I definitely recognize the Frodo impulse that says, "Let's pretend this doesn't exist." We do a lot of learning together about racial injustice and white privilege in my predominantly white community, and a common reaction of folks (and men, especially) is to say, "I see the problem now! I recognize my privilege and the social power that has been handed to me, and I don't want it." *Power* becomes a bad word.

But the reality of social power dynamics is that if you are the high-ground person in the room, regardless of how many times you try to ignore the power you've been given or pretend it doesn't exist, *it does exist*. MaryKate Morse talks about this at length in her book *Making Room for Leadership: Power, Space and Influence*.[1] She says when any person walks into a room, the other people in the room (subconsciously) are factoring in that person's power and influence. We unknowingly assess key things like race, gender, personality (introvert versus extrovert), economic status, role, education, marital status, dress, and so forth. Imagine that for every factor that puts you on higher ground, you are given an imaginary bean. Those with the most beans in the room are typically granted the most influence by the people in the room.

Now, imagine that the person in the room with the most beans says, "I don't have any beans" while they're holding a giant handful of beans! Imagine they even thrown the beans on the floor and neglect them. Does that help any of the people in the room? Does that change anything for the people with fewer beans? Does it lead to a healthier dynamic in the group where power is being shared? I would argue that it doesn't. The same social dynamics that handed beans to the powerful person in the room is just going to keep handing that person more beans, keeping them out of the hands of the people with fewer or no beans. What would it look like, instead, for those with more beans to persistently and intentionally distribute the beans to other members of the group? I say "persistently" because it's not something that can be done once and for all; it needs to happen repeatedly and consistently.

When people who are privileged with more power recognize that privilege and power, the answer is not to disown
that power or pretend it doesn't exist. Instead, it is to open
ourselves up to the kind of formation we need to steward the
economics of that power well within our community.

This is the kind of learning we are grappling with in my
church community. I find one of the things I need to do well to
pastor the men in my congregation is to encourage them not to
"check out" from their privilege, but to own it, not in a way that
uses it for their own purposes and preferences, but in a way that
says, "I have this resource; help me understand how I can offer
this to the group. I can't figure it out myself. I need your help."

BRANDON: I've had an eclectic church experience growing up.
In each setting my interaction and understanding of power
were very different. I grew up in the Church of God in Christ
(COGIC), so my initial understanding of power was always
something that we needed as a people, something that was
imparted to us, that moves us, but not something we possessed. Power wasn't something we were able to wield; it was
what moved us. This theology was always coupled with various
forms of social outworking. The pastor held the most power
in that he was more proximate to the divine by the nature of
his call. However, he was held in check by the same power that
entered each of us. There was this spiritual accountability as it
relates to power. There was this unspoken adherence to a philosophy that we—as the dispossessed—are as powerful as we
are connected to God, and within our own echo chamber
there was this silent and steady belief that our time was coming
when we will be lifted up.

But as we spoke about power in the context of society at large, it was something to be overthrown and equalized through the coming of God's kingdom. The thought was that if we instill kingdom values in work spaces and in social spaces, then power would be equalized and our inevitable ascension would be actualized. Power in this community is leveled out to a degree largely because of the cultural and socioeconomic homogeneity and the fact that many of those who attended our church lived in the neighborhood. There was a oneness, a corporate sense of place and identity. It made it easy to give confessions because whatever you confess as a struggle would be accompanied by groans of resonation. Whatever seemed to be an obstacle, whether relational or civic, was a shared struggle or at least one that felt accessible to the community. If sister McCarthy had her electricity cut off, there wasn't shame or a sense of being less than associated with it, because everyone in the space at some point had experienced that, and they relied on the community to get out of it. There wasn't a hierarchy. When it came to our economic realities or social mobility, America's patriarchy and racist infrastructure made our reality a common denominator.

The church of my youth is distinctly different from the church I currently attend, in that the commonness of the struggle is no more. The more diverse the community, the more apparent power and our understanding of power seems to be. It is in the multicultural spaces that power seems to be the most apparent and damaging.

I don't think it's any less damaging when people understand the context in which we do church. Even when folks are "woke," power is present and most pervasive in these spaces. I think this happens for a couple of reasons.

Power can go unnoticed. When it is in conflict—when it is challenged—it makes itself known. It manifests itself in our perceived norms and in the disorientation that comes when the norms are challenged by the other.

In our context, we make a concerted effort to identify those points where power will manifest itself and the ways we need to steward it. However, our approach to measuring and articulating power is done in a way that may give credence to the system of power we are ferociously trying to dismantle. There is verbiage and perceived norms that serve to validate whiteness and maleness as the baseline. For example, we even structure our learning in a way that uses white ignorance as our point of departure. Most race-and-power conversation starts with the push to have whites and males to—in good conscience—relinquish power. Which almost never happens. Even when they give up power, they do so on their terms. Versus calling the marginalized to demand liberation and to accept nothing less, to call all of us to a higher kingdom-minded form of revolt.

Second, wokeness can in itself be a form of consolidating power. Woke white voices are extremely damaging at times. They master rhetoric and police behaviors which don't always deal with internalized implicit biases. Their racist instincts lie dormant until catalyzed by threat. And so many of our woke friends are internally wrestling with institutional, socially formed ideologies under the guise of being woke. On the surface, our woke allies can present an environment of humility and transparency. I call it the rich-young-ruler syndrome. When we can make the "gospel of wokeness" attainable by religious efforts, we can at times find our woke friends saying, "I have kept all of the law," but when circumstances or an encounter with Jesus asks them to sell all they possess— which in this case may be the mantle of wokeness itself—we see many of our brothers and sisters walk away downcast. We are at our best when we simply build posture rather than right behavior, because a constant posture of humility will produce right actions.

ADAM: I resonate with that. On the one hand, the problem of trying to bury the power I carry does nothing to dismantle the larger injustices of oppressive power. If my level of discomfort or naiveté regarding the power I wield makes me want to bury it, nothing changes in the dynamics of our community. The people under the thumb of power continue to experience its marginalizing effects while I continue to move through the world unencumbered. On the other hand, it's possible to use *being aware of racism and injustice* as a stiff-arm against God working his justice out in and through my life.

I wonder if we could press in even more here and ask for you to share about ways you've experienced the *backside* of power within the congregational context. Can you give some examples of ways you watch or experience leaders (particularly white or male) wield power in unhealthy ways? How does that undercut the work of justice? How does it get in the way of cultivating a shalom community?

JULIET: The thing that comes to mind first is how our first response from a high-ground place of privilege is always to want to fix the problem or fix the injustice using our own methods and sense of what would be right and helpful.

Our church exists within a denomination that does not affirm women in pastoral ministry, yet our local congregation does affirm and call women into every level of ministry (which is why I am a pastor there). I remember a late-night church meeting where we were expressing frustration together at the inequity we see in our denomination. One of the men in the meeting took over and basically proclaimed a plan: "This is what we need to do: A, B, and C . . ." Without consulting any of the women in the room about how they felt or if they had any intuition or thoughts about what needed to happen, he took over the situation and heralded his way of fixing the problem. Rather than being empowering, he was actually disempowering the women in the room—the very opposite effect he intended to have, I'm sure. While I understood his heart and appreciated his willingness to act, there was some maturity that needed to grow in the way he approached his own power.

I'm learning that we always need to ask, "Is this empowering others, or is this taking over and disempowering others?"

I'm an Enneagram Two—a "helper" by nature—and so I include myself in this! I often want to be helpful by doing things for others, proposing what I think is best and following that plan of action. But I can get in the habit of steamrolling people to get things fixed. I've learned I need to slow down, listen, ask the person or people what they think is best, offer my insights or opinions with openness and humility, and hand over power to them.

ADAM: I am increasingly nervous about the attempt to use worldly power against the agents of injustice in the world. This is not to say we never use power, but appropriating the tools and tactics of oppressive power for the ends of liberation only extends the problems we long to see redeemed. It's hard to wield power for good. That feels like what you are describing, Juliet. I often notice the tendency to separate myself from the unjust situation (I'm innocent of this) and to also want to jump in and solve the problem. Maybe that's something particularly common for white males, something I'm trying to learn to be aware of in my own life. Thanks for bringing that up.

As I think about it, learning to steward power well is a process rather than a result. How would you articulate the journey of learning to steward power (for people who occupy historic positions of power) more faithfully?

BRANDON: In continuing my previous answer, humility. One would think this would be easy for the church, seeing as though our entire worldview is built on a premise that we are fallen people, that in our natural state we see things wrong. So the idea that we might be askew should not be such a shock. All have sinned and fallen short of the glory of God—this line of thinking should make it acceptable to assume that our use of power, our view of the other, our view of ourself might be sinful as well. To the degree that we can buy into this theology, we can experience appropriate stewardship. We first have to say we aren't doing this right: "Please, someone help me do it right." It's like any other cycle of sin. When we think we can free ourselves from it, that's when we find ourselves spiraling deeper and deeper. We rely on self-deception and build communities that buy into our false realities, protecting ourselves in echo chambers of ignorance.

When we become open to being naked and called out and forgiven and loved and accepted, we can begin to steward power.

Our instincts are jacked up, so we will always need this accountability. But it begins with embracing something we claim to believe already—that we don't see it right. And then we need to move to spaces of others who agree that they don't see it right as well. All the while acknowledging power, holding that power before the community and asking, "What do I do with this?" Like other forms of discipleship, it requires a *walking with*; it cannot happen with self-actualization alone.

ADAM: Can you point to examples of power used well?

JULIET: One way my church community is learning to use power well is through our practice of shared leadership and communal discernment.

When our congregation is facing theological disagreement or uncertainty, rather than having the leaders dictate "from on high," we invite the community into the process of learning, reading Scripture, sharing stories and experiences, and praying together. Over time, we hear from each other and listen for how the Spirit is at work.

To determine how we are engaging our neighborhood and seeking the shalom of our community, we don't determine this on the pastoral team. Instead, we see our jobs as pastors to listen to members of our congregation. We ask them, "What is God showing you in your neighborhood, place of work, school, or family? What injustice would God notice from your past week? What do you see him doing—and how are you joining him in that work? What can you celebrate about the place God has put you in? What grieved you this week in that place?" As pastors, we look for patterns and themes to emerge that might give us a sense for what God is doing in us together.

When we have noticed something, we offer it to the congregation, exploring if there is resonance in the community.

We also have a copastoring model; instead of a senior pastor, three of us (myself and two guys) copastor together. We share the tasks of ministry, but copastoring is more than delegation; it is the practice of communal discernment as a way of leading together. This slows things down. I can only imagine that top-down leadership can feel more fast and efficient. But we find that we are being formed by this in ways that I don't imagine I would need to be formed in a top-down, hierarchical setting.

For us, this means we are doing cross-gender and cross-cultural ministry together. I am an Asian American woman pastoring with two white males. We're all different Enneagram types and Myers-Briggs. Trust me, we've encountered a lot of frustration, conflict, difference of opinion, and talking past each other. The gospel is worked out between us in the midst of all these things. It takes hard work—it is truly a dying to oneself! I am challenged by my copastors' differences, and they are by mine. But we believe this is a beautiful embodiment of the kingdom of God.

BRANDON: Regarding an example of power used well, I would say River City's staff decision-making process. We do almost everything on a consensus basis; there is no decision being made without buy-in from all the staff. This makes the process long and arduous, but it really leaves no room for a fall guy. When we fail, we fail together. When we succeed, we succeed together. The important aspect of this philosophy is to have a truly diverse team—diverse in almost every sense of the word. Theological, denominational, ethnic, gender, racial, and political diversity coupled with a belief that there can be "nothing about us without us." This is the belief that there can be no decision made about a group or individuals without their participation in the process.

Our process is far from perfect. It is flawed and inefficient, but the intention is to mute power and steward it in a way that benefits the collective.

ADAM: I'd be interested in your take on how power affects the issues we discussed earlier in this book. How do you see power intersect with the idea of church as prophetic alternative and parable of God's intent seeking transformation and flourishing?

JULIET: Part of the witness we offer as a prophetic-alternative community is the way we share power and steward it for the good of the whole, rather than one type of people. This is why one of the foundational things about my church community is that communal discernment is a way of life together.

So, it's imperative to become good listeners in community as well. It's easy to come up with the ways we think flourishing and transformation need to happen. But are we listening to our neighbors and asking them for their ideas?

ADAM: What about in our day-to-day life as a congregation: vision casting, building community, corporate gatherings, and the like?

JULIET: Vision always begins in and among the people, never from above. A couple of years ago, we began seeking God's will for our church's vision. We started by asking every member of our congregation, How have you experienced God's work in your life here? What do you see him doing here already? What longings do you have for our future together? The leadership (pastors and elders) accumulated all these responses and looked for themes to emerge.

Also these are the practical ways we seek to move from *I* to *we*. We meet in the round each Sunday. We face each other in this space. The Communion Table is at the center, so we see each other *in light of* who Christ is and who he is making us. This helps us as we think of all of our life together in these categories: living in Christ, with one another, for God's mission in the world. Our copastoring model is a subset or microcosm of the greater community, where we model sharing discernment and power, humbling ourselves to encounter difference and be formed, learning mutuality and partnership. We then also use a benevolence fund to which we can give to people among us who fall into hard times and need financial help.

BRANDON: Amen to all Juliet said here! I do want to mention that I do not believe there is sin in being a homogenous group of people. I didn't find my all-black congregation lacking. Our homogeneity was a result of social design, not one of exclusion. Of course, there are things we just didn't know and couldn't have experienced, and an ignorance that comes with that. But by in large we were a humble, hospitable, welcoming community.

That being said, the impact power has is determined primarily by the vehicle power occupies. Power in our context occupies race and gender and so on; the various spectrums of power that flow from the "host" make the stewardship of power an issue of diversity and inclusion.

The work of the church to steward power will ultimately have us manage the "host" that power resides in. Our work feels shortsighted if we just develop an orthodoxy of race and gender relations, which I think is necessary but not comprehensive. Our theology most go deeper, to the places where power and the pursuit of power find their origins. Power can occupy the mantle of wokeness, it can reside in what it means to do church "right," it can reside in all forms of political correctness. Because of its corrosive nature, power is so pervasive it can find itself in our corrective measures.

Our only real guard against it is a constant position of humility and the flexibility to change when we get it wrong. That is why I believe smaller congregations have a better shot at working these things out. Humility requires that we remain attentive and nimble. In smaller communities, voices are louder, and it's harder to have folks lost in the shuffle. And when we need to pivot, we can.

ADAM: It's interesting you say that, Brandon, about the size of the congregation. Both of you have very perceptive insights on the internal machinations of power within congregational life, and both of you work in congregations small enough to know most of the people and observe the work simultaneously at the individual and corporate level. This makes me wonder what we might lose once we get to a certain size congregation, and if perhaps the dynamics of power become impossible to discern and steward because we fall into more impersonal systems that resist the kind of extra labor involved in creating a community that seeks to steward power faithfully in community. I'll be chewing on that for a while.

POWER IS THE LINCHPIN

Power is the linchpin of justice. Good intentions do not overcome an unhealthy power dynamic. Good theology can't on its own deal with patterns of abuse of power. Good justice initiatives in the community will not automatically unearth the corruptive nature of power mishandled in the local church. If we do not get this right, we will always struggle to become just churches. By *get it right* I don't mean to conclude that there is a silver bullet. Instead, getting power right is going to be a question of posture, process, perspectives, and voice. Posture is a way of being in community related to power. The process will be ongoing, and so patterns have to be established to regularly grapple with power. The issue of perspective is needed because good postures and process will be undermined if the filter used to understand situations is still seated with one privileged person or group. It is also about voice. I suppose I could have said access, seat at the table (or even reframing whose table it is, to begin with), or authority. Ultimately, the ones we empower—as a community—to lead us will be gatekeepers, and so who those people are will be a critical issue if we hope to cultivate a community where power aids the work of justice rather than hinders it.

I learned many of these lessons the hard way as a young pastor in a community of multiethnic congregations in New York City. Pastoring a mostly white, English-speaking congregation in intentional collaborative community with Chinese and Arabic congregations, I saw my work, partially, as laying bare the realities of power in the pursuit of a relational covenant to work out together.

That meant creating space over time for me and those who looked like me to identify, name, and resist unhealthy impulses. It meant doing hard work to understand the collateral damage of our naive use of power, and in community across ethnic and cultural lines, to discern a more faithful expression of the kingdom. It was a bumpy process moving along in fits and starts, but my time in this community taught me that the work of justice had to emanate from the character of our community and the internal issues related to power and leadership.

One of the most consistently difficult conversations we had was in the area of ministry to youth. Because the majority of our young people were English-speaking Chinese immigrants, our youth ministry overwhelmed our congregations in complexity. We had to learn to identify and acknowledge the way the power dynamics between these groups influenced our process of discernment. In moments when we tried to pretend that power dynamics were irrelevant, people quickly retreated to antagonism and distrust. As we were able to own our dynamics and confess our missteps, we were able to carve out a deeper level of mutuality in ministry than I initially thought possible.

This is the kind of work we are going to have to do in our congregations, particularly those who are predominately white. The layers of power at work in our life together are many, nuanced, and subtle. It is crucial that we develop eyes to see and Spirit-sensitized ways of discerning together how we might resist unhealthy uses of power in favor of a way of life that is genuinely mutual and capable of becoming a community that functions well as a body under the one head of Christ. This is a thread that weaves through everything we've discussed so far and will likely be the single-most determinate factor in our ability to cultivate communities of God's shalom.

EPILOGUE

COMMENCE JUSTICE

The stories and statistics are staggering.

As I write this, families are being torn apart, punitively, at the border—a cruel "deterrent" against illegal immigration. These are children, some infants, removed from the custody of their parents; many came seeking asylum from the threat of violence in their native countries. This is every parent's worst nightmare: to flee for the safety of your children only to have them stolen from you when you arrive at the very place you came seeking refuge.

But the church is a people who follow Jesus, who, like many of these little children, fled in the arms of his parents to escape politically motivated violence. Jesus was a refugee, the first-century equivalent of an accompanied minor seeking asylum. What an opportunity for the church to demonstrate the prophetically *other* nature of its identity by simply standing where Jesus stood.

Mass incarceration is shredding black and brown communities across the country. The rate of incarceration in the United States—overwhelmingly for nonviolent drug crimes—is greater than any nation's in the history of the world.[1] Yet an egregious number of these offenses come as the result of unjust disparities in sentencing guidelines that unequivocally fall along racial lines. What many refer to as the criminalization of black and brown bodies has been happening since this nation's inception. The systematic delegitimization of these bearers of the divine image is part of our cultural DNA.

But since the church is a parable of God's intentions—the demonstration of God's tomorrow—it would seem we are poised to extend a radically *other* way of life into a world. This other way of life would not only show but also invite the watching world into a deeper reconsideration of its status quo for the sake of extending the experience of God's transformative shalom to the margins we have created and continue to codify through policy and preference of certain types of people over others.

The number of ways our world finds to dehumanize, to oppress, to marginalize, and to extract the real possibility for a free and flourishing life from the most vulnerable are innumerable. The effects of poverty, violence, discrimination, and structural inequity have saturated our society, and when we look the other way we find ourselves complicit in the perpetuation of the worst of what our world has to offer.

Confronted with the reality of our society, it is tempting to disregard Martin Luther King Jr.'s assertion that "the arc of the moral universe is long, but it bends toward justice" as pie-in-the-sky foolishness. And while some may interpret it that way, Dr. King's words reveal an imagination soaked in the eschatological hope of the kingdom of God. There is no other way to make sense of these words. If we think that the world will just *eventually* become just, we are kidding ourselves. The only way to stand behind such a phrase is to locate ourselves squarely in the streams of the eschatological proclamation of Jesus, the one making everything new again. It is only through this lens of God's *tomorrow* that he could make such an audacious claim in the midst of a devastatingly unjust *today*. Jesus is making everything right, good, true, and whole again. If that is not true, then this book is folly and our pursuit of God's shalom is a chasing after the wind.

Without the eschatological hope of God's kingdom, it is naive to believe Dr. King's words. It puts a blind faith in the capacity of humanity to find and maintain a moral center we've spent thousands of years hiding under the rug. I don't fault the optimism of those who hope to find an alternative path to a more just and human society. I love them for it, actually. It is evidence of our collective, deep-seated yearning for a world more fair, free, and just. The same way everyone who meets my kids recognizes their mother's eyes in each of them, this resonance with the shalom of God is the mark of the divine DNA in each of us and in the communities we are on this earth to create and cultivate.

Yet without churches who are increasingly cultivating God's shalom in their midst, these impulses and resonances with the things of God go untranslated for the wider world desperate for respite from the onslaught of ugliness and injustice that we see and experience day-to-day. Without the radical story of Jesus who came to proclaim freedom and favor for the poor, the only way we can believe in the eventuality of justice is to put our faith in the shaky capacity of society to right itself.

I believe it is the responsibility of every church, irrespective of context and social location, to weave the pursuit of God's shalom *as a way of life* into the cultural fabric of the congregation. Without it, we are not fully the church.

I am all for church planting. But if these church plants are not fully rooted in a community, bearing the fruit of God's shalom justice, then can we say that we faithfully planted *a church*? I am also a sucker for a dramatic conversion story. Seeing the younger brother come home to the father is a momentous occasion and worthy of celebration. But if we are calling "come home" to these siblings but forgetting to show them the actual way home, or the real meaning of giving up one's life for the sake of Jesus, then what are we celebrating? I can affirm the value of the spiritual practices in the contemplative life. But spiritual practices *aimed at what*? What kind of life do we seek to help people find? I am for the work of justice, obviously. But if we distance ourselves from the church—God's determined mode of extending his kingdom shalom to the world—what are we accomplishing, really?

These are questions that find fuller expression in the church committed to becoming a community of God's shalom. That means the kind of people we are, together, matters. The way we orient ourselves in the world, the things we pursue, the way we go about navigating life in community, shape the collective character of our witness. The God who is tomorrow is defined by the total transformation of the broken injustice of the world, and his fruitful and flourishing shalom invites us to discover anew the incredible way of being his people in the world.

And this way of life in the world takes seriously the eschatological reality framed by Dr. King's words regarding the arc of the moral universe. Only the church can offer a definitive and resounding amen to such a sentence. Only the church lives into and out of a story in which that is fully true. Only the church can cultivate a Spirit-empowered way of life in the world that demonstrates—authentically and tangibly—what the end of the story Dr. King points us to actually looks like.

So, what story are we telling?

COMMENCE JUSTICE

It's strange to me that graduation ceremonies are officially called "commencement." Except that the ending that is graduation is really a beginning, commencing the very thing the season of schooling has been preparing a person for. The issue is I never really think of graduation in that sense. In all of my graduations, I've never seen it as a beginning. Just the relief and jubilation of a job well done (theoretically).

I wonder if that might the same with justice for some of us evangelicals. Rather than seeing an awakening to injustice and discovering God's heart for shalom as a commencement, we see it as a job well done. And so we might fail to get to the actual *work of seeking justice* because we sense that we have made it and accomplished what needed to be done.

I suppose that is one of my fears with this book, in writing it and the way it's organized. Because it's possible to read this book and think, *Well, if we wrestle with these things, we have done what we need to do. We have leaned into our calling to be the church as it relates to justice.* Of course, the perceptive reader will have noted that even if every piece of this book was applied (and that's assuming a lot about the veracity of the content, anyway) in the local context, the church in question will have done little to engage the issues of injustice, inequality, and marginalization. This is a book about the *long game* of becoming a particular type of people. It's a course correction for generations who have drifted away from the heart of God's shalom. But we cannot wait to get our face right to engage the faults of society.

In other words, the work of public justice is still to be done. And it would be a mistake to use the work of cultivating just communities to resist that work. It is true that partisan politics can't save the world, and the election of a leader isn't the coming of the kingdom. But that doesn't mean it doesn't matter. The call to love our neighbors well, to pursue their flourishing as bound up with ours, necessarily means that we will find ourselves tangled up in the mess of the world's political systems and structures.

This book is written on the premise that we need a way of being the church that makes sense of our calling as the people of God so we can pursue God's justice in the world without being co-opted by the right or left, without being corrupted by the vain motivations of our consumer society, and without falling prey to the temptation of using the world's tactics as we seek God's kingdom ends. We have done so little of this work well over our history as evangelicals that I fully appreciate the instinct to withdraw—from the church or from politics—and the assumption that we cannot do the public and political work of justice without becoming corrupted.

The answer, though, is not extraction from political engagement. The reality is that our most vulnerable friends and neighbors, the ones who occupy the low ground of society, experience a structured kind of injustice that will in the end require engagement with the political powers in order to seek authentic justice. Issues like immigration, community policing and mass incarceration, SNAP benefits and economic policy, local zoning, education, and lending practices will require direct engagement in the political process to meaningfully stand in solidarity with our neighbors and advocate for a more holistic view of a thriving community. To reject these issues—calling them outside the purview of the church—is an abdication of the responsibility of co-heirs of Christ.

I believe this is work we can engage in faithfully without becoming beholden to the powers of American politics (even if we aren't very successful at this these days) *and* without diminishing our commitment to *being* a just people ourselves. In fact, these pursuits cooperate with one another. As Alexia Salvatierra and Peter Heltzel argue in their fantastic book *Faith-Rooted Organizing*, "Congregations are unique in the U.S. movement for justice in that they maintain two simultaneous purposes—working to change the broader community while also becoming a model community."[2]

As I close, I want us to wonder together about what political engagement might look like flowing out of a way of being the church we've been wrestling with all along. It makes me think that the central plank in the platform of a *just church* could be that *our political views and actions arise from the lived experience of our neighbors at the margins*. Given the priority of Jesus (and then the church) to center the folks who occupy the social low ground, and the radical way the pursuit of authentic kinship creates an opportunity to demonstrate the shalom justice intentions of God, it seems natural to conclude that our political engagement should be driven by an overwhelming focus on the flourishing of our neighbor, particularly those most vulnerable to being trampled on by the structural machinations of an unjust society.

This calls for a priority on a local and embodied political witness. To take seriously the lived experience of our neighbors at the margins means that politics is not based on issues but in people. We will have to recognize that any issue of political concern is so precisely because it involves the real lives of real people. In our translocal way of consuming the political dialogue, news, and narratives, it is easy for us to fall into ways of thinking about politics divorced from real life. When we know neighbors who deal with a broken immigration system, the collateral damage of incarceration, or the inequity in public education, we are no longer free to deal with ideas in abstraction. Instead, because we are committed theologically and ecclesiologically to the flourishing of our neighbor and the transformation of our neighborhood, each issue we engage is decidedly *embodied* in the lives of those we live with in community. We are now free from the pressure to label, demonize, and exclude; we are free instead to love our neighbors as we love ourselves and as a tangible expression of our love for God.

Concretely, we allow the pain of our neighbor to shape our passions and priorities. Allowing the shattered shalom of our friends and neighbors to drive our agenda will challenge us to engage the local work of politics as a high priority. The temptation, of course, is to constantly get swept up into the national political drama and rhetoric, but we would do well to remember that much, *much*, of the potential impact we have is most effectively worked out through local political structures.

- We advocate for shalom for our neighbors in city-council meetings and by organizing efforts for a more vibrant, livable community for everyone.

- We demonstrate our concern for health care by leaning into local efforts for affordable clinics and prescription-drug access.

- We work with local business associations to help our entrepreneurial neighbors gain access to small business start-up coaching and investment.

- We invest our time and resources in local schools and with the school board itself to ensure that every child in the neighborhood has an equitable educational experience that sets a trajectory for a life of wholeness and flourishing.

- We build collaborative partnerships with law enforcement, not only to make our most vulnerable neighborhoods safer but to enhance accountability with policing practices.

I could go on and on, but the point is to emphasize the way our commitment to living locally and for the sake of the flourishing of our neighbors who have been pushed to the margins will get worked out even in a political sense.

The work of public justice is a natural and needed overflow of the work of becoming a just people ourselves. If the lines between congregation and community are blurred in a healthy way, and the church is in meaningful and authentic relationship within the neighborhood—a community of friends and neighbors—then this will be the most obvious outworking of the way of life for the church. Indeed, churches across the country have embodied this kind of life in community for generations.

The evangelical church has catch-up to do, but it is not an impossible task. We need to listen to the voices of folks who have lived and labored in communities wracked by injustice, poverty, and violence. Voices of leaders from the margins will lead the way for us as we seek to recover a new or renewed faithfulness.

So let us be just. Even as we seek to do justice. May we not forget that becoming a certain kind of people in the world gives us the capacity for a certain way of life *in the world*. It does not stop in the becoming. We must commence justice.

ACKNOWLEDGMENTS

Writing this book, I was reminded time and again of the great gift of being part of God's people in a particular place and time. I'm incredibly grateful to the people of First Evangelical Free Church in Brooklyn, New York, and River Valley Church in Mishawaka, Indiana, for their trust and patience with me as a pastor as we sought to work out what it means to be the church in the place God put us.

I've had amazing pastors, teachers, collaborators, guides, and teammates over the years who have challenged and shaped me as a pastor and helped hone my vision for the pursuit of justice in the church. Ben Dodd, Andrew Gates, Bill Redekop, Grace Mo, Safwat Attia, Roy Larsen, Lisa Yeung, Jeremy Del Rio, Lee Eclov, Matt Tebbe, J.R. Briggs, Juliet Liu, Dave Clark, Bethany Harris, Stephen Kriss, Christena Cleveland, David Swanson, Jose Humphreys, Daniel Hill, Brandon Green, Cecilia Williams, Dominique Gilliard, Christine Moolo, and Paul Hawkinson are a few names among a great cloud of saints who have left their imprint on this book in many ways.

Throughout my life, a few folks radically changed the trajectory and perspective of my work, and I am indebted to each of them for showing me a way of life that is truly life: David Whited, Greg Leeper, and Peter Cha at Trinity College and Trinity Evangelical Divinity School; the late Manny Ortiz, Sue Baker, and my DMin cohort at Biblical Seminary; and Dennis Edwards, an incredible mentor, pastor, and friend in the journey.

Thanks to Al Hsu and the team at InterVarsity Press for your faith in this project and your help along the way. This is an infinitely better contribution to the world because of the life you brought to it.

South Bend, Indiana, is forgotten by many, but I am daily inspired by the army of shalom seekers there. Their passion for God's justice showing up in the lives of actual people and actual places is commendable. Together, we are learning how great and wide is the love of Jesus, and I cannot wait to see the paths he gives us to work it out together for the sake of a city he loves.

Finally, my family. I'm grateful for their support and encouragement in the writing of this book and throughout my life. Thank you to Josiah, Levi, and Nina for putting up with many early mornings and weekends when Dad was holed up writing, and to Ann for your help in the process and your unshakeable belief that there were words inside me that were worth putting on paper. I don't always see what you see, but knowing you see it helps me step into the world and seek God's shalom. William Blake said that "we are put on this earth for a little space, to learn to bear the beams of love." As someone for whom the beams of love are still often ill-fitting, I have a long road of learning ahead of me. What a gift to share this space with Ann, who bears them so well. She embodies the shalom of Jesus and watching her lay her life down for the other takes my breath away. Thanks be to God for her.

NOTES

INTRODUCTION

[1]Bono, keynote address at the 54th National Prayer Breakfast (Washington, DC, February 2, 2006).

[2]Carl F. H. Henry, *The Uneasy Conscience of Modern Fundamentalism* (Grand Rapids: Eerdmans, 1947), 10.

[3]This is common language for this conceptual framework. I first heard it from John M. Perkins at a CCDA training event in Chicago in April 2014.

1 JUSTICE ISN'T AN OUTREACH STRATEGY

[1]Eugene Cho picks up on this notion when he argues that God will use the work of justice to "challenge us, change us, and transform us.... [W]e need to pursue justice not just because the world is broken, but because we're broken too" (Eugene Cho, *Overrated: Are We More in Love with the Idea of Changing the World Than Actually Changing the World* [Colorado Springs, CO: David C. Cook, 2014], 51-52). In later chapters, we will explore the possibilities for discipleship available to us when we more fully integrate justice into our life together.

[2]David Fitch, *Faithful Presence: Seven Disciplines that Shape the Church for Mission* (Downers Grove, IL: InterVarsity Press, 2016).

[3]Fitch, *Faithful Presence*, 13-14.

[4]Martin Luther King Jr., "Letter from a Birmingham Jail," in *I Have a Dream: Writings and Other Speeches That Changed the World*, ed. James M. Washington (San Francisco: Harper, 1992), 85.

[5]Melba Padilla Maggay, *Transforming Society* (Eugene, OR: Wipf & Stock, 1996), 3.

[6]Maggay, *Transforming Society*, 4.

[7]Stanley Hauerwas and William H. Willimon, *Resident Aliens: Life in the Christian Colony* (Nashville: Abingdon Press, 1989), 33.

2 EXILES IN THE PROMISED LAND

[1]Dennis Edwards notes, "An identifying mark of God's ownership of the Christian community is its distinction" (Dennis R. Edwards, *1 Peter*, Story of God Bible Commentary [Grand Rapids: Zondervan, 2017], 102).

[2]"Foreigners . . . are often held at arm's length, as they are typically viewed with suspicion and have an unstable position within the dominant culture" (Edwards, *1 Peter*, 102).

[3]Stanley Hauerwas and William H. Willimon, *Resident Aliens: Life in the Christian Colony* (Nashville: Abingdon Press, 1989), 17-18.

[4]Brueggemann, *Prophetic Imagination*, 2nd ed. (Minneapolis: Augsburg Fortress, 2001). 3.

[5]Hauerwas and Willimon, *Resident Aliens*, 74.

[6]Al Tizon, *Missional Preaching* (Valley Forge, PA: Judson Press, 2012), 52-53.

[7]"Both [conservative and liberal political Christians] assume wrongly that the American church's primary social task is to underwrite American democracy" (Hauerwas and Willimon, *Resident Aliens*, 32).

3 DEMONSTRATING MAÑANA

[1]Eugene Peterson, *The Contemplative Pastor* (Grand Rapids: Eerdmans, 1989), 32-33.

[2]Justo González, *Mañana: Theology from a Hispanic Perspective* (Nashville: Abingdon Press, 1990), 163.

[3]González, *Mañana*, 164.

[4]"Mañana is most often the discouraged response of those who have learned, through long and bitter experience, that the results of their efforts seldom bring about much benefit to them or to their loved ones. . . . [M]añana is the response of farm workers who realize that no matter how hard they work, most of their income will end up back in the hands of the employer; or of the tenement dweller in New York who knows that efforts to improve living conditions will most likely be erased by slum lords, drug traffickers and even city ordinances" (González, *Mañana*, 164).

[5]González, *Mañana*, 164.

[6]González, *Mañana*, 166.

[7]Stanley Hauerwas and William H. Willimon, *Resident Aliens: Life in the Christian Colony* (Nashville: Abingdon Press, 1989), 38.

[8]Al Tizon, *Missional Preaching* (Valley Forge, PA: Judson Press, 2012), 55.

[9]Tizon, *Missional Preaching*, 55.

[10]Lesslie Newbigin, *The Good Shepherd* (Grand Rapids: Eerdmans, 1977), 20.

[11]Serena Solomon, "Meet the Woke Young People Trying to Make Christianity Cool Again," *Vice*, November 3, 2017, www.vice.com/en_us/article/j5jjgb/meet -the-woke-young-people-trying-to-make-christianity-cool-again.

[12]"The . . . church can participate in secular movements against war, against hunger, and against other forms of inhumanity, but it sees this as part of its necessary proclamatory action. This church knows that its most credible form of witness . . . is the actual creation of a living, breathing, visible community of faith" (Hauerwas and Willimon, *Resident Aliens*, 47).

[13]For more on this notion of seeing beauty and brokenness see the conclusion of Jonathan Brooks's *Church Forsaken* (Downers Grove, IL: InterVarsity Press, 2018), 201ff.

4 GARDENERS OF SHALOM

[1]Dennis Edwards, "Flourishing," *CCDA Theological Journal*, ed. Soong-Chan Rah, Chanequa Walker-Barnes, and Brandon Wrencher, 2014 ed. (Chicago: CCDA Publishing, 2014), 14.

[2]Jonathan Brooks, *Church Forsaken* (Downers Grove, IL: InterVarsity Press, 2018), 177.

[3]"In the *Torah*, prosperity and blessing are measured by how well the destitute poor, fatherless, immigrants and widows are faring in the neighborhood. . . . True prosperity and flourishing in Scripture is always rooted in an awareness of our vulnerability as created and redeemed by God. It is a partnership with God in the embrace of the more vulnerable. . . . The measure of a truly rich community is the condition of the local poor" (James K. Bruckner, "Prosperity and Witness: A Biblical Witness," *CCDA Theological Journal*, ed. Soong-Chan Rah, Chanequa Walker-Barnes, and Brandon Wrencher, 2014 ed. (Chicago: CCDA Publishing, 2014), 6-7.

[4]Eric Reis, *The Lean Startup* (New York: Crown Business, 2011).

5 LOW-GROUND CHURCH

[1]See Abdallah Fayyad, "The Criminalization of Gentrifying Neighborhoods," *Atlantic*, December 20, 2017.

[2]David P. Leong, *Race and Place: How Urban Geography Shapes the Journey to Reconciliation* (Downers Grove, IL: InterVarsity Press, 2017), 146.

[3]Leong, *Race and Place*, 147-48.

[4]"Life together as Christians simply cannot function under the authoritarian demands of cool. Communities of color have repeatedly paid the price for occupying the unenviable position of living at the shifting margins of the city, and . . . while it's true that some forms of urban ministry have arguably become cool for some, once the exoticism of poverty wears off, there's very little cool about the slow and difficult ministry of working incarnationally against the structural injustice in the city" (Leong, *Race and Place*, 148).

[5]"If we follow the geography of grace in cities, then one place I believe we'll find ourselves is not primarily with the 'movers and shakers' above us, but 'underneath the bridge with the moved and shaken'" (Leong, *Race and Place*, 144).

[6]In *Geography of Grace*, Kris Rocke and Joel Van Dyke say, "Grace is like water—it flows downhill and pools up in the lowest places" (quoted in Leong, *Race and Place*, 143).

[7]"*Marry and have sons*. . . . Echoing the first responsibility of humankind during Eden's unadulterated state, God calls Israel to be fruitful and multiply" (Allie Wong, "Cities of God: Reclaiming Culture Through the Flourishing of the City," in *CCDA Theological Journal*, ed. Soong-Chan Rah, Chanequa Walker-Barnes, and Brandon Wrencher, 2014 ed. [Chicago: CCDA Publishing, 2014], 36).

[8]"*Build houses and settle down*. The first charge leads presumptuously with a certain degree of permanency: establish a geographical foundation in Babylon. . . . [W]hat was countercultural in this mandate was to reject attitudes and actions of transiency" (Wong, "Cities of God," 35).

[9]Jan Milic Lochman, "The Lord's Prayer in Our Time: Praying and Drumming." in *The Lord's Prayer: Perspectives for Reclaiming Christian Prayer*, ed. Daniel L. Migliore (Grand Rapids: Eerdmans, 1993). 18-19.

6 RECOVERING KINSHIP

[1]Boyle, Gregory. *Tattoos on the Heart: The Power of Boundless Compassion* (New York: Free Press, 2010). 187.

[2]Boyle, *Tattoos on the Heart*, 187.

[3]Boyle, *Tattoos on the Heart*, 189.

[4]Julia Dinsmore, *Seeking Shalom* (Atlanta: Lupton Center). *Seeking Shalom* is a six-part video curriculum.

[5]Donald McGavran and C. Peter Wagner, *Understanding Church Growth* (Grand Rapids: Eerdmans, 1990).

NOTES TO PAGES 131-198

[6]Christena Cleveland, *Disunity in Christ: Uncovering the Hidden Forces that Keep Us Apart* (Downers Grove, IL: InterVarsity Press, 2013), 48-49.

[7]Dietrich Bonhoeffer, *Life Together* (New York: Harper & Row, 1954), 36.

[8]Ana Maria Pineda, "Hospitality," in *Practicing Our Faith: A Way of Life for a Searching People*, ed. Dorothy Bass (San Francisco: Josey-Bass, 1997).

[9]Pineda, "Hospitality," 33.

[10]Dinsmore, *Seeking Shalom*.

[11]Henri Nouwen, *Reaching Out: The Three Movements of the Spiritual Life* (New York: Doubleday, 1975), 66.

[12]Boyle, *Tattoos on the Heart*, 189.

7 FINDING COMMON KINGDOM GROUND

[1]Eric F. H. Law, *The Wolf Shall Dwell with the Lamb* (Danvers, MA: Chalice Press, 1993), 71-77.

8 WORSHIP

[1]"Lament in the Bible is the liturgical response to the reality of suffering and engages God in the context of pain and trouble." Soong-Chan Rah, *Prophetic Lament: A Call for Justice in Troubled Times* (Downers Grove, IL: InterVarsity Press, 2015), 21.

[2]Rah, *Prophetic Lament*, 21. Rah continues to unpack in more depth the modern evangelical resistance to lament. Helpfully, he connects that resistance to the relative comfort some have with a status quo that preferences them. We might not lament because we see nothing worth lamenting. His stellar treatment of the theology and practice of lament is well worth reading.

9 POWER

[1]Mary Kate Morse, *Making Room for Leadership: Power, Space and Influence* (Downers Grove, IL: InterVarsity Press, 2008).

EPILOGUE

[1]Dominique Dubois Gilliard, *Rethinking Incarceration: Advocating for Justice that Restores* (Downers Grove, IL: InterVarsity Press, 2017), 27.

[2]Alexia Salvatierra and Peter Heltzel, *Faith-Rooted Organizing: Mobilizing the Church for Service to the World* (Downers Grove, IL: InterVarsity Press, 2014), 93.